The Financial Affairs of David Lloyd George

David Lloyd George: 17 January 1863 – 26 March 1945
(© Shutterstock)

The Financial Affairs of David Lloyd George

Ian Ivatt

welsh academic press

Published in Wales by Welsh Academic Press, an imprint of

Ashley Drake Publishing Ltd
PO Box 733
Cardiff
CF14 7ZY

www.welsh-academic-press.wales

First Edition – 2019

ISBN
978-1-86057-125-1

British Library Cataloguing-in-Publication Data.
A CIP catalogue for this book is available from the British Library.

Typeset by Prepress Plus, India (www.prepressplus.in)
Printed by Akcent Media, Czech Republic
Cover design by Siôn Ilar, Cyngor Llyfrau Cymru, Aberystwyth
Cover image ©Press Association

Contents

Welsh Place-Names
Author's Note

Wales has changed significantly since the days of David Lloyd George. One very visual example of this has been the replacement of the anglicised spellings of place-names – i.e. Carnarvon, Criccieth, Portmadoc and Nevin – with the original Welsh versions – Caernarfon, Cricieth, Porthmadog and Nefyn – and I have endeavoured to accurately reflect this change by using the contemporary and linguistically authentic Welsh place-names throughout the book.

However, for the sake of historical accuracy, when referring to specific organisations, institutions and the electoral divisions that existed during Lloyd George's life, I have used the official names from that period i.e. Carnarvon Boroughs.

To three remarkable individuals – Jacqueline, Mary and Graham – and, separately, the Open University.

Introduction

With the possible exception of Winston Churchill, David Lloyd George has been the subject of more published works by biographers and historians than any other British political figure. The bibliography section of this work is evidence of the frequent examinations of his political and private life, which have been published over many years. This dates from Herbert du Parcq's 1916 volumes, right up to more modern analysis by both Dr. J. Graham Jones and Roy Hattersley's 2010 books. Ffion Hague's carefully crafted work of 2008 on Lloyd George's personal life, entitled *The Pain and the Privilege*, equally comes to mind. Lloyd George and his financial affairs have, to date, not really surfaced in any strong way save for some interesting references to the Patagonian gold fiasco, as sizeably covered in John Grigg's 1973 work *The Young Lloyd George*. In contrast, this book, *The Financial Affairs of David Lloyd George*, pays little heed to the great man's politics, nor indeed his numerous dalliances outside of his marriage to the equally admirable and courageous Maggie, his long-suffering wife. These present studies emanate from earlier research degree work on the Liberal Party in southern England, and were flavoured from time to time by Lloyd George's appearances and visits to Sussex. The connection with this county, which is my own home county, repeatedly cropped up by his fascination with Brighton, the fact that two of his children, Olwen and Gwilym, were educated in Sussex, and his love of the game of golf on the nearby Lewes links. This made me, a confirmed Southerner, want to explore more about this unusual man from north Wales. I had, therefore, effectively joined the band of Lloyd George devotees. In this process, when on one of my research trips to the National Library of Wales in Aberystwyth, I had the extreme good fortune to meet Dr. J. Graham Jones, the well known Lloyd George author and expert. He immediately and unstintingly gave me his advice and guidance, and I was immediately struck by his enthralling vision and enthusiasm for the subject. In simple terms, I too became smitten with Lloyd George and, five years ago, we discussed the question of Lloyd George's financial life – a subject in specifics, which had not received any real level of probing analysis. This book is intended to fill that potential void and, hopefully, provide another insight into Lloyd George's activities by way of money dealings, share purchases, newspaper acquisition and, really breaking new ground, it contains fresh information in detail about his fruit farming and associated horticultural endeavours after he lost power in 1922. He then, literally, planted his roots in southern England in a most interesting property called Bron-y-De, just outside the Sussex county boundary, almost where the counties of West Sussex, Surrey and Hampshire intersect, in the village of Churt, near Farnham. I was additionally fortunate to track down possibly Lloyd George's (or at least Frances Stevenson's) child, Jennifer (1929-2012), and spent time with her, a few years ago, discussing the great man and filling in some of the gaps in my existing information. Indeed, Lloyd George was much irked by any criticisms both of a private and political nature; the former put to the test in a financial context by the remark attributed to the editor of the *Manchester Guardian* (see Chapter 2) that Lloyd George was not a great devotee of money. There are some quite contrasting pieces of evidence here, as the forthcoming pages will reveal.

This book attempts to address one basic question, at least on financial terms; that is to say, how did the relatively non-wealthy indentured pupil of a north Wales solicitor manage to reach the heights of Prime Ministership of Great Britain, with the inherent financial benefits. Clearly David Lloyd George's widowed mother, Elizabeth (or Betsy) George (1828-1896), must take the initial credit here for she was the one whose dwindling capital resources managed to pay for his, and indeed his younger brother William's, training expenses to enable them both to qualify as legal practitioners in the law of the land. Equally, once Lloyd George (to some extent with his new bride, Margaret's, misgivings) had been elected to Parliament in 1890 by the slender majority of only eighteen votes, he was able to mix with more affluent members of the House of Commons, which enabled him to reflect on how he might move up the money scale, especially as ordinary MPs were not salaried at all until 1911. Balanced against this was Lloyd George's general dislike of inherited wealth, or at least, the comforts and privileges that such money bought. His admiration, in contrast, for self-made men was paramount. Consequently, relatively quick and easy money-making schemes had appeal – almost anything that would assist in the meeting of pressing domestic and family expenditure. Additionally, there was the great sacrifice made by William George in running the family legal firm, Lloyd George and George, back in north Wales and the business profits, which enabled Lloyd George to remain at Westminster for over fifteen years before he began to be paid as a Cabinet Minister in late 1905. This was crucial, and Uncle Richard Lloyd also devoted some time to help run the legal business. Without their wholly selfless sacrifices, Lloyd George simply would not have been able to remain a Member of Parliament for this length of time with no Parliamentary salary.

This study additionally encompasses questions over funds required to meet urgent and unexpected personal costs, when gold is not all that glitters; an introduction to share ownership and dealing; inheritance of assets; newspaper proprietorship; life assurance arrangements; and of course the (by now) well known Marconi share and sale of honours scandals. The chapter dealing with Lloyd George's horticultural interests includes newly researched information about crop yields, manurial benefits, bee-keeping and honey yields. This has resulted from the study of a whole box of privately held records dating from the late 1920s, 1930s and just into the 1940s, which were made available to me in early 2014 and provided an additional economic insight into the viability of the entire fruit-growing business, retail outlets, and what was undertaken on only part of the entire 850-acre estate. These pages will portray, where relevant, a financial analysis of the great man, not always establishing an undisputed answer to the money issues thereby covered, but providing some underlying reasoning and background to such aspects.

As a chartered tax accountant, I am familiar with financial terms and patterns, and thus felt more than adequately equipped to cover this largely untapped part of the Lloyd George life story. My heartfelt thanks go to Dr. J. Graham Jones for his ongoing interest and kindness and to Dr. Neil Riddell for his valuable overview. Equally I must also thank, especially and strongly, the almost magical and enthusiastic support given to me by my late wife Jacqueline, who sadly lost her battle with cancer in early 2015, and to my best friend, and new wife, Mary, for her undeniable patience and advice on layout, wording and production. Without these four, I am sure my work would have almost foundered. Finally my thanks must go to the Open University for giving me the opportunity to hone my research skills and in general terms the interest shown by their experienced academics.

Ian Ivatt
Steyning, West Sussex
April 2019

Foreword

David Lloyd George (1863-1945), the last Liberal to serve as Prime
Minister of Great Britain, from 1916 until 1922, is already the subject
of more than sixty biographies of varying merit as well as numerous
more specialised studies and an array of articles in academic volumes
and journals. Of twentieth century national politicians, Winston
Churchill alone has attracted greater scholarly attention and more
publications.

The story of published biographies of Lloyd George by now extends
back to a little over a century when John Hugh Edwards published
his pioneering volume *From Village Green to Downing Street* (1908),
soon to be followed by the same author's substantial four-volume
biography of *The Life of Lloyd George*. Herbert du Parcq published a
similar multi-volume biography in 1912, a still immensely useful
work. These early biographers were generally sympathetic and
admiring to their subject, as indeed were slightly later writers like
the journalists Harold Spender and E.T. Raymond in the early 1920s.
The dramatic fall of Lloyd George from power in the autumn of
1922, however, led to a marked change of emphasis which became
apparent in the generally hostile, critical works of biographers like
J.A. Spender, A.G. Gardiner and, above all, Charles Mallet – all of
these disgruntled, embittered Asquithian Liberals.

After Lloyd George's death and the end of the Second World War in
1945, a number of important biographical works appeared, including
full volumes by Sir Alfred T. Davies (1948), Malcolm Thomson (1948)
– the official biography prepared with the full collaboration of the
Dowager Countess (Frances) Lloyd-George of Dwyfor and unrestricted
access to the papers in her custody bequeathed to her by Lloyd George
– and Frank Owen (1954). A pioneering volume published by Lloyd
George's long-suffering Principal Private Secretary, A.J. Sylvester, *The
Real Lloyd George* (1947) also portrayed the former Prime Minister
in rather a bad light as 'a soured, autocratic and peevish old man'.

Even greater hostility was, predictably, apparent in a biographical volume by Lloyd George's elder son Major Richard (Dick), the second Earl Lloyd-George of Dwyfor, which appeared in 1960. A previous biographical volume written by 'Dick' Lloyd-George about his mother in 1947 and entitled *Dame Margaret* was, equally predictably, much more sympathetic and, indeed, idolatrous. Generally critical, too, was the tone of Donald McCormick's outspoken study *The Mask of Merlin* (1963). And this attitude of criticism was also perpetuated in the more general works of historical interpretation published in the first half of the 1960s.

From this point on, however, a more sympathetic, revisionist, rehabilitation-orientated attitude emerged to Lloyd George, reflected in the works of several eminent historians like Martin Gilbert, Cameron Hazlehurst, Robert Skidelsky and Peter Clarke. This was in part the result of the availability of exciting, new primary source materials, notably the magnificent archive held at the Beaverbrook Library (later transferred to the custody of the Parliamentary Archive at the House of Lords), and the so-called Brynawelon group of papers purchased by the National Library of Wales in 1969 from the estate of Lady Megan Lloyd George. In consequence, important source works flowed from the press – extracts from Frances Stevenson's diary in 1971, *Lloyd George - Family Letters 1885-1936* and a selection of the letters between Lloyd George and Frances Stevenson in 1975. The first volume of John Grigg's outstandingly accomplished multi-volume biography *The Young Lloyd George* saw the light of day in 1973, to be followed in due course by three further substantial, authoritative volumes which take the story down to the end of the First World War. Two further volumes planned by Grigg were, sadly, never completed before his death in 2002. A similar long-term project by a distinguished American historian, Bentley B. Gilbert, yielded two impressive volumes, but the series came to an end in the year 1916. The deaths of both these biographers brought these promising series to a sadly premature end. Important thematic works included Chris Wrigley's *David Lloyd George* and *The British Labour Movement: Peace and War* (1976). A massive, comprehensive single-volume biography was published by Peter Rowland in 1975 and has generally stood the test of time. Lloyd George's only nephew, the late Dr. W.R.P. George of Cricieth (1912-2006), published in 1976 and

1983 two important works which traced his uncle's career down to his entry into the Cabinet in December 1905, and based primarily on the superb archive of private correspondence and papers then in his private possession, subsequently purchased by the National Library of Wales, or the one in London.

Thereafter there ensued something of a brief lull in Lloyd George studies, but deep interest has certainly revived during the last decade or so, when a spate of seminal works has seen the light of day. These include major works from the pen of John Campbell, Richard Toye, Ffion Hague, Roy Hattersley and Travis Crosby. Further significant biographical works by Richard Wilkinson and Huw Edwards, the newscaster and broadcaster, await publication in the near future. The celebration in January 2013 of the 150th anniversary of the birth of Lloyd George and the mounting of memorial exhibitions have also led to a renewed interest and some re-assessment of his many lasting achievements and towering contribution.

In this important pioneering study, Ian Ivatt has focussed his attention on a key theme previously rather neglected by historians and biographers of Lloyd George – his relationship with money and financial resources throughout his life and career, an absorbing subject for a study of this kind. Throughout his public life, Lloyd George liked to claim that his background was highly deprived and poverty stricken. Certainly, a visit to Highgate (now an appendage of the Lloyd George Museum), the local cobbler's humble cottage in the small rural village of Llanystumdwy, near Cricieth, the home of Lloyd George's uncle and adoptive father Richard Lloyd (1834-1917), where the future Prime Minister spent his formative years, is sufficient to demonstrate that the family was far from wealthy or well resourced. On the other hand, their material existence was comfortable by the standards of the age, and family members did not generally want for anything. Lloyd George's mother Betsy experienced some financial bad luck, and belts certainly had to be tightened in order to finance young 'Davy' George's legal education and training together, a little later, with similar provision for his younger brother William (born in 1865). Even after Lloyd George had set up his own legal practice, work was, initially, often slow to come in, and money remained tight. To some extent, marriage in January 1888 to Maggie Owen, the only daughter of the well-heeled and influential Richard and Mary Owen of Mynydd Ednyfed Fawr, Cricieth, provided the ambitious young attorney and aspiring politician with potential access to far greater resources (although under the ever-watchful eye of his suspicious and interfering in-laws, who had both rather resented the marriage).

A new chapter certainly opened in all their lives when the twenty-seven-year-old Lloyd George, rather earlier than anticipated, was elected – by a hairsbreadth majority of just eighteen votes (1963 to 1945) – to the House of Commons in a snap by-election in April 1890 as the Liberal MP for the highly marginal Parliamentary constituency of the Carnarvon Boroughs. At the time (and indeed right through until 1911), backbench MPs received no Parliamentary salary whatsoever. They even had to pay their personal travelling expenses, often substantial, between Westminster and their home constituencies. This situation inevitably led to severe financial difficulties for the Lloyd George family. For a long fifteen and a half years – until he eventually entered the Liberal Cabinet in December 1905 – Lloyd George's sole constant source of income was the sometimes scant profits of the family legal firm, Lloyd George and George, conscientiously nurtured by his younger brother William and, to some extent, by Richard Lloyd. His only other income was the occasional fees which he received for political articles contributed to journals and newspapers. Lloyd George was, indeed, as John Grigg put it, 'excessively beholden to his brother'.[1] His combined income from law and journalism as reported to the Inland Revenue in the year 1893 was a modest £338 and thus likely to cause material hardship.[2] The need to juggle his multifarious constituency engagements, London-based political activities and legal work on occasion, vexed him sorely. On more than one occasion during the long 1890s, Lloyd George seriously considered abandoning completely his promising political career to earn his living as a full-time lawyer, as his wife Margaret wished, or else to apply for the Bar, as many of his friends and associates urged. Ultimately, in 1897, he resolved to establish a second solicitor's business at 13 Walbrook, London, in partnership with Arthur Rhys Roberts, a native of south Wales, previously an assistant solicitor with Ward, Colborne and Coulman of Newport, Monmouthshire, and already engaged in legal work in the great metropolis.

Their financial situation was transformed at the end of 1905 when Lloyd George, his patience exhausted, at long last attained Cabinet rank as President of the Board of Trade with a relatively high annual salary of £2,000, later to be increased to an annual £5,000 when he succeeded Asquith as Chancellor of the Exchequer in April 1908. By this time, too, Richard and Mary Owen were both in their graves, presumably having bequeathed a substantial real estate, including property, to their adored only daughter. The Lloyd Georges' new-found opulence was reflected in the construction of a grand, expansive family home called Brynawelon (hill of the breezes), overlooking the town of Cricieth and the rolling countryside round about, and in their ability to finance a comfortable lifestyle at various London homes for part of the year. They were even able to send their children to prestigious English public schools, a costly commitment over several years. Thereafter a substantial ministerial income was assured – until Lloyd George fell from power, as it happened for ever, in the autumn of 1922. Thereafter his sole political income was the £400 annual salary paid to backbench MPs by that time. During his long tenure of 10 Downing Street, he had taken every opportunity, presumably for the most part through the 'sale of honours' and other privileges, to accumulate a substantial war chest known as the Lloyd George Political Fund which, by his fall in 1922, it is estimated ran to several million pounds. Its very existence, and the tight restrictions which he invariably placed upon its use, proved a severe bone of contention for the rest of Lloyd George's life. After his ejection from the premiership, he was able to command a substantial income as one of the most highly paid journalists in the whole of Europe and, to a lesser extent, as an accomplished public speaker and lecturer. He also became involved in potentially lucrative newspaper ownership. Two main financial themes dominate the long 1930s – the publication and sales of Lloyd George's mammoth six-volume *War Memoirs* between 1932 and 1937, and the relentless building up and development of the expansive estate at Bron-y-De near Churt in the Surrey countryside, a hugely successful enterprise, diversified into both animal husbandry and horticulture – notably apples, raspberries and honey – and eventually employing about a hundred individuals, including numbers of 'land girls' during the Second World War. Towards the end of his life Lloyd George also purchased and developed an old Georgian farmhouse by the name of Tŷ Newydd in Llanystumdwy, where he was to breathe his last on 26 March 1945.

All these compelling, engrossing themes, central to an understanding of Lloyd George's life, are dissected with a masterly touch by Mr. Ivatt. He has spared no effort to master the ever burgeoning published literature on David Lloyd George, has waded through the various scattered archival sources and scoured the newspaper columns too. He has also conducted personal interviews and undertaken research on the ground. His researches are also provided with a unique cutting edge by his own personal expertise as an accountant. All his enthralling discoveries have been deftly welded into a cohesive, absorbing account of the financial interests of a man who, in Churchill's immortal words, was 'the greatest Welshman that unconquerable race ha[d] produced since the age of the Tudors ... When the English history of the first quarter of the twentieth century is written, it will be seen that the greater part of our fortunes in peace and in war were shaped by this one man'.[3]

J. Graham Jones
Aberystwyth
April 2019

Notes

1. John Grigg, *The Young Lloyd George*, (Methuen, London, 1973), p.175.
2. Ibid., p.174.
3. Cited in Robert Blake and William Roger Louis (Eds.), *Churchill: a Major New Assessment of his Life in Peace and War*, (Oxford University Press, Oxford, 1993), p.6.

'Lloyd George's conversion [to Bank of England ways] was a triumph, but he himself is really a wonder. It took some time to teach him but he promises now to reach the front rank of financial experts, if his present knowledge makes him retain a taste for the pure finance side of Treasury work which he has hitherto entirely neglected'.

Treasury Official, (Sir) Basil Blackett,
8 August 1914

'In ordinary times one can spare time and tissue to soothe the vanities and jealousies of civil servants who magnify their offices – but these are not ordinary times'.

Lloyd George to Financial Secretary, Edwin Montague,
in January 1915

89

At a Meeting of the Life Committee,
held at Nº 1 Moorgate Street
on Thursday, 10ᵗʰ January 1895

Present,
Colonel Baring, in the Chair,
Mr Lubbock,
Mr Lucas,
Sir Algernon West
The General Manager,
The Actuary.

The following Proposals were reported disposed of
since last Meeting, and the papers relating to the same
were laid upon the Table and examined by the Committee

Accepted.

Birmingham	W. H. & A.B. Black	£250.	Ordinary Premium
Brighton	F. Jones	1.000	Dº
Birmingham	J.S. Wright	500	Dº
Dº	F. W. Stockley	200	Dº
Dº	J Foley	200	Dº
Manchester	M. Sharples	200.	Dº
Birmingham	H Bentley & N. Ellison	500	Dº
Dublin	J P. McMurray	500.	Dº
Dº	A.G. Fitt	500.	Dº
Direct United States Cable Cº	J. Wilson	100.	Dº
Manchester	W. P. Johnson	600.	Dº
London	S.J. H. W. Allin	200	Dº
Birmingham	S. Wilkes	2,000.	Dº
Helsingfors	A. H. W. Vageler	400	Dº
Newmarket	H.O. Sharp	500.	Dº
Bristol	A. C. Games	200	Dº
Dº	Y. H. Mills	500.	Dº
Birmingham	D. Lloyd-George	1.000	Dº
Dº	H. D. Stratton	250.	Dº
London	F. Duffell	200.	Dº
Town	A. Hill	250.	Dº
Nottingham	J. W. Bloore	100	Dº
African Direct Telegraph Cº	F. R H. Jardo	200	Dº
Birmingham	D. V. Johnstone	500.	Dº
Dublin	S. McLarmon	100.	Dº

Lloyd George listed as an insurable risk with Northern Assurance, January 1895. (See Appendix 2 for details)

1

1863-1888
A Lawyer in the Making

'Of tireless energy, fervid eloquence, and indomitable courage, he was possessed by a burning sympathy for the 'underdog' and a fixed determination to remove the injustices under which they suffered'.
Rufus Isaacs (1st Marquis of Reading)

David Lloyd George (1863-1945), according to A.J.P. Taylor, was 'The greatest ruler of England since Cromwell'. Undoubtedly, he did not fit in, or belong to any particular category. Save for Winston Churchill, Lloyd George is in all probability the most written about politician, with many accomplishments, a master of social and political events and, in reality, not a firm political party dogmatist. As we shall see, he rose from humble (but not outrightly poor) beginnings, to become, after other earlier Cabinet positions, the successor to Herbert Henry Asquith, the Prime Minister of Great Britain.[1] Much has already been published and culled, from the numerous books already penned, from diaries, archive material and personal recollections, on the subjects of his political achievements, disappointments, family feuding and, relatively recently, his relations with women. Yet, no serious attempt has been made, until now, to examine, assess and analyse his attitude to money and finance in general – both by way of receipts and expenditure. Indeed, there is a story to tell about a man who, after a basic education at a national school, started work as a trainee solicitor's clerk, at fifteen years of age in 1878, to earn 15 shillings (less than £40) by way of commission for collecting insurance premiums from householders in Porthmadog for the principals of his professional firm – to compellingly compare with the probate valuation on his death, on 26 March 1945, of £139,855 (nearly £6.5 million pounds now).

As Lady Violet Bonham Carter once remarked, 'Lloyd George was saturated with class consciousness',[2] whilst his friend, working colleague and devotee, Churchill, was not (yet he remained a fundamental aristocrat by conviction, laced with an added touch of opportunist social reform concepts), although Lloyd George's views were essentially geared to opposition of landlordism,[3] and inherited wealth. Conversely, the Welshman was drawn to self-made, financially successful entrepreneurs and businessmen, including newspaper barons.

Equally, by not going to any university or college, he broke the mould of earlier British Prime Ministers. Professor Kenneth Morgan's 1974 book opens with a description of Lloyd George 'as a rogue elephant amongst British Prime Ministers'. Contemporaries called him 'the big beast', and there have been many other equally apt descriptions of the man, more recently to conclude with Lord Hattersley's 2010 publication entitled *Lloyd George – The Great Outsider*. Lloyd George was accorded all this variable flattery, and more, and this particular examination will seek out whether such descriptions can be similarly applied to his monetary and financial dealings.

It was usually Lloyd George's claim that he originated from a background of some poverty. Always one to exaggerate his 'cottage bred' upbringing founded on much-reduced circumstances; yet was this really true? The family budget was stretched, but potatoes, home-made bread, cheaper cuts of meat, sometimes buttermilk, jam and even butter were available – it was a case of waste not, want not that was the order of the day. Nevertheless, Lloyd George always maintained he came from an impoverished background, yet this oft-repeated concept needs to be challenged. Obviously, losing his father William George when not yet two years of age (with an elder sister, Mary Ellen, born 1861 and a brother, William, as yet unborn) and his widowed mother Betsy having to move the family from Bulford Farm on the North Pembrokeshire coast in south Wales to Highgate Cottage in the village of Llanystumdwy, near Cricieth,

Caernarfonshire, in north Wales, was a disruptive start to life by any standards. Yet, to Betsy's brother's house, Highgate, they came, to add to Richard Lloyd's household, including his mother, the resourceful and determined Rebecca, and the George children's grandmother. Money was certainly not plentiful, although as an economic unit, the occupants of Highgate were one of the better-off family groups in Llanystumdwy village. Betsy brought with her her late husband's collection of history and academic books, assets, and net savings, by way of the sale proceeds from the Pembroke leasehold home, in all a total of about £768, then held mainly in the Liverpool Building Society. W.R.P. George adds that the total figure included furniture sales of £34, farming stock £57, lease, and crops of £64 and £90 rent arrears outstanding from their tenant. This in itself brought in interest income of £46,[4] being somewhat better than some local agricultural workers' likely annual income.

Their landlord, Dafydd Jones, the village shop keeper, owned the majority of houses in Llanystumdwy, and was not famed for paying for any repairs to his tenanted homes; his argument was founded upon 'the house is yours, the rent is mine!' thesis. Thus house repair and maintenance expenditure fell upon Richard (uncle) Lloyd, or Betsy George (previously Lloyd), actual rent payable being £7 per annum.[5] Nevertheless, Richard and Rebecca (who died when Lloyd George was only five years old) did run a boot repairing business from the adjacent single storey stone-built workshop with, at one stage or another, up to three or even four paid assistants. Brother William George's account on likely income receipts of the business, up to 1857, reveal that, undertaken on three household work benches, boot making and repairs costed out at 10 shillings a pair of men's boots, 8 shillings and 6 pence for women's boots, whilst a pair of soles were charged at 2 shillings and 6 pence. Thus, Uncle Lloyd laboured for six days a week, Rebecca undertaking paperwork tasks and debt collecting, whilst Betsy ran the household. On the seventh day, the Sabbath, Uncle Lloyd undertook the role of unpaid pastor of the Campbellite Baptist Sect, worship being conducted in the chapel on the hill behind nearby Cricieth.

Betsy's domestic and economic skills were exceptionally good, aided and abetted by the reliable Rebecca; the children were always well dressed, with both David and William wearing knickerbockers, socks, and caps – not the usual apparel of working class labouring families. Undoubtedly, the Georges were not well off as such, and financial hardship arose from time to time, but in reality, the children, Mary Ellen, David and William, did not effectively want for anything. David Lloyd George, or Davy Lloyd as he was now beginning to be known, loved to tell a tale to eager listeners of his boyhood, where the three George youngsters had to share an egg between them each Sunday, to demonstrate a level of frugality. William George, his brother, pours cold water on this yarn; 'I certainly never remember any such dramatic performance taking part in any meal of ours at Highgate'.[6]

Davy's allotted family tasks were the upkeep of the garden and the collection of firewood from local woodlands, to develop his green-finger skills under his mother's direction, which was to prove vitally useful, some decades later, when David Lloyd George personally owned hundreds of acres in Surrey devoted, with the assistance of legions of employees, to fruit growing and arable crops. William's tasks included organising the buckets of water each day for family use, whilst Mary Ellen (or Polly, as she was now called) greatly assisted her mother with baking, cleaning, washing and general housework. Even so, Betsy was proud enough not to let her two boys join in with the other village lads for weed picking at gentry homes, usually with the earning potential of sixpence a day. Quite simply, Betsy undertook a brave, even heroic fight to bring up her children on a respectful and fair basis.[7]

Indeed, both the George brothers were fortunate in their school days, not just benefiting from their father's treasure trove of good, instructive books to read, but by receiving a first class basic education (from the age of three years and seven months in Davy's instance) at the Llanystumdwy National School, courtesy of the excellent school master, David Evans. Young Davy, whilst excelling at the 'three Rs', geography, history, English and later algebra and Latin, would never be happy at this Church of England school with its establishment focus on English literature, history and geography, the English language and of course Church of England religion. At least 80 per cent of village parents that sent their offspring there were actually non-conformists! Also, any Welsh history, language and literature was ignored. As W.R.P. George explains, the effect was, 'a regime calculated to engender a rebellious spirit in a Welsh non-conformist child, with an independent outlook on life. This is exactly the effect that the school had on the young boy, Davy (Dafydd) George'.[8] Nevertheless, two aspects of his school days are worth noting, namely his handwriting which was, all his life, difficult to understand and, secondly, a special feature of this school which ensured that navigation and seamanship were taught to older and ex-pupils who became sailors in the merchant fleet based in nearby Porthmadog Harbour. Both these concepts have a bearing on Davy's future, namely his almost unreadable manuscript in his lifetime, and financially, as will be seen, in the area of ship ownership by his later kith and kin. However, in these early stages, Lloyd George's handwriting was neat and tidy, but it became virtually unreadable, and certainly more untidy as time went on, especially as he later obtained Cabinet rank – worse still during the First World War.

Meanwhile, Davy's mother, Betsy, still juggled with her limited income to cover the household costs of three growing youngsters. At one stage, Betsy asked the Liverpool solicitor and family friend, Thomas Goffey, to review earlier records as regards the possibility of any belated financial claim on the old Pembrokeshire property; alas, nothing new was discovered. Nevertheless, Goffey, evidently, was still very well thought of (especially as he was reputed to earn a respectable £300 per year) and was sent, despite fluctuating but regular returns on the invested building society, a plump, well-plucked Llanystumdwy turkey each Christmas, an annual drain on the George family finances. However, Davy, brother William and sister Polly who had been despatched (only for about a year as it transpired) to a private school in Cricieth to learn deportment for girls of the middle and upper working classes, aided the household economy each autumn by gleaning corn from the reaped fields as permitted by local landowners. Indeed, one year provided enough free corn for the brothers to take to the nearby Felin Fach flour miller, the resultant flour being given to Betsy to bake delicious bread.[9]

Betsy, whose health by the mid-1870s began to be a big concern because of asthma, did not wish to depend more than was necessary on her own brother's tentatively successful boot and shoe business, however willing he was to share. In particular it was noticed how indispensably helpful Richard was to the two George boys, educationally speaking, especially Davy, who was the 'apple of his eye'. Much has been written about Richard (Uncle) Lloyd being a surrogate father to young Davy and there is no denying his lasting influence on the boy, covering religious, learning, and paternal areas. He himself had a vast grasp of biblical happenings and events, and his clear undertaking in life was to ensure Davy Lloyd's success in the world. Brother William must have been envious but showed little, if any, evidence of such an emotion.

At the time of Davy's school leaving in 1878, plans had to be made for his future, and conceivably the final decision was based upon some subtle direction from the much-respected Mr. Goffey of Liverpool or possibly from Davy's frequent visits as an observer to the Wednesday Petty Magistrates' Courts sessions in neighbouring Pwllheli, or even both. Therefore, 'it was decided in family conclave that Davy was to become a lawyer'.[10] The cost of such a step, initially, by way of the usual indenture premium and stamp duty would amount to £180 (about £15,000 today); the reliable Mr. Goffey proposed the amount be funded from Betsy's invested capital. The said £180 was paid over just after Davy's sixteenth birthday in January 1879. This 'loss' from the investment would obviously mean less or lower payments of interest on the remaining capital sent to Betsy. Of course, the situation would be repeated, as it transpired, when the younger brother William went down the same career path. Thus, in the summer of 1878, young Davy, now professing to be called David Lloyd George, began his first work in the Porthmadog offices of Messrs. Breese, Jones and Casson, on an initial six-month trial basis. Family, mutual friends and religious connections played their part in making the necessary introductions. The firm's solicitor principal, Mr. Edward Breese, was a Liberal, a regular churchman, and at election times acted as an agent for the Liberal candidate in the adjacent constituency of Merioneth. This was very much in accord with David Lloyd George's perceptions, with the added proviso that if David was so minded to take the Law Society Preliminary examinations (and pass, which he did) it would be arranged for him to be articled to one of the firm's partners, Randall Casson. Moreover, in view of David's young age, Edward Breese agreed to retain a fatherly and personal interest in the boy. David was to obtain lodgings, at a cost of 10 shillings a week, in Porthmadog at David Owen's house, a local auctioneer, during the working week and to return to Highgate Cottage, Llanystumdwy, on Sundays. David Lloyd George had made his life's first real venture into the law, and indirectly into politics, which would later become the great calling of his life.

David Lloyd George's career, as an articled clerk, now comprised of becoming familiar with all the legal day to day business of the office, namely using shorthand, witnessing deeds, creating leases, engrossing mortgages and undertaking a whole range of other legal requirements for many, including the law firm's largest client of Porthmadog town and harbour, Tremadog Estates, whose previous sole proprietor, W.A. Maddocks, had died in 1828. Added to this, David was obliged to take his Intermediate Law Society examinations, which meant much evening candlelit reading and regular weekend study sessions, with, of course, the ever-attentive Uncle Lloyd looking on and encouraging the young man. This included mastering the French language, which the treasured uncle had to learn first.

The Welsh country practice of Breese, Jones and Casson had, as has been intimated, a much varied client base and the one task that befell the young articled clerk was collection, each half year, of the Tremadog Estates' leasehold tenants' fire insurance premiums. It was a tedious requirement for David and, later, his brother William, George. As any lowly articled clerk rapidly discovered, the benefit was obtaining a greater knowledge of Porthmadog's townsfolk, businesses and personalities. Additionally and equally relevantly, once this thankless task had been completed, and the books balanced by the firm's cashier Mr. Holl, there was a gratuity of 15 shillings, payable to the lucky clerk.

Thus David's career progressed, heightened by a few clear hints from his solicitor principals to improve his office and legal skills, together with his own diary notes of self-chastisement of 17 and 24 September 1879, 'my mortgages untidy – [I] must be better', and 'let me try to make myself more affable towards everyone ... Clients are not gained by a hitherto thou-shalt-come-and-no-further mien and attitude, think on it'.[11] It would not be too extreme to claim that his famous 1909 Budget proposals, as Chancellor of the Exchequer, were based on the principles and experiences of his articled clerk's working days.

Indeed, young David Lloyd George's working experiences also led him to the actual port facilities of Porthmadog, and this involved talking to ships' masters and crews – spellbound by their seafaring stories. The subject of ships and vessel ownership would, as implied before, involve his future wife's parents. Equally, now aged over fifteen, he tended to have an eye for the fairer sex that plays no part in this study, plus he was very respectful or at least paid lip service to Uncle Lloyd's religious temperance and high moral standards. Even so, Sunday was reserved for worship and David undoubtedly appreciated his uncle's regular Baptist sermons. David's diary entry for Sunday 17 November 1878 states, 'R[ichard] Lloyd – his climax splendid, conversational, then grand'.[12] David's employment progressed well, a mixture of professional legal services and evening studies, the latter with the untiring and strict Uncle Lloyd as his mentor. Economically, young David's life and indeed the life of his immediate family were still being stretched. Betsy's weekly cash allowance to her son, David, which including his lodging costs at the Owens', did not really go far enough. Also, Uncle Lloyd's shoe and boot business, now without the influence of Rebecca, was winding down to a virtually negligible state, resulting in little or no money now going towards household expenditure at Highgate Cottage. With Betsy's own building society interest being reduced from the lower capital base, together with a strong possibility of repeat expenditure when brother William embarked upon the same professional career, the future did not look financially bright. Some changes were necessary.

The decision to move house was therefore reached, exchanging the expense-ridden rented Highgate Cottage, for the similarly rented, larger, but less costly to maintain, Morvin House in Cricieth, in May 1880. The new landlord was the Cricieth hardware dealer, a Mr. G.P. Williams, who, from the goodness of his heart, occasionally lent money to Richard Lloyd. In the same month, David escorted his brother William to Beaumaris to sit (successfully) the preliminary law examination. After a family debate, David gave up his lodgement with the Owens in Porthmadog and rejoined the family at Morvin House in June of that year. No more money allowance to David, thought Betsy, and no more lodging fees to fund either. Conversely, Uncle Lloyd's business had now effectively ceased, due to the maestro's failing health. Nevertheless, he lived until 1917. Yet, not so good for David was that he now came under the constantly watchful eye of his vigilant uncle again. For David, this meant a walk to work and back from Porthmadog at five miles in each direction. Yet, David had other ideas, not just confined to evading his uncle's and, occasionally, his own sister's lecturing for late-night timekeeping and flirting, but also as an alternative to his ever time-consuming studies for his Law Society final examination, now scheduled for late 1881. From late 1878 Williams' *Real Property* and Hallam's *Constitutional History of England* were being eagerly absorbed, with David writing a detailed synopsis of Williams' writings.[13]

The seventeen year old's interest now very much embraced politics. His absorption with political life was beginning to ferment such enraptured thoughts that there was more to just becoming a country solicitor, and politics could expand his horizons to a higher, quite possibly national, platform. David reasoned that, as his hero, Abraham Lincoln, had emerged from an almost identical background and had got to the top as a national figure, then so, quite potentially, could he. Understanding, as his brother faithfully records, that it was the 1880 General Election (and later the Caernarfon County by-election in that same year) that first fired David's curiosity and with it especially political thoughts of freeing society from the landlord, the Anglican parson and church, gentry and aristocratic influences. In his life as an articled clerk, David spent time additionally in the local law courts, witnessing procedures and judgments, in readiness to prepare himself for the next set of Law Society examinations, which were to be held in London. Meanwhile, the unexpected death occurred of his initial solicitor principal, Mr. Edward Breese, following an accident whilst shooting game, and this greatly saddened David, as he felt morally reliant on Mr. Breese and later, in almost the same way, towards Mr. Randall Casson. Nevertheless, David needed to put money aside to meet examination costs, in the clear knowledge that his family's financial structure would not fund a second attempt if he were to fail. Odd moneys from friends and relatives were most welcome in this respect and David's own diary records of 5 November 1881, reflect, 'Wm. Williams of Manchester House called and gave me £2 towards my scheduled journey for London'. This was a magnificent gift.[14]

The year 1881 turned out to be a very important one in David's life as employment, politics and journalism all came into focus to run alongside his ever-demanding studies towards the vital Solicitors

Intermediate examinations. Whilst the (Lloyd) George family's move to Morvin House, Cricieth, had minimal immediate benefits, aside from there being more space, finance, or at least the perpetual challenge to curtail expenses, gained enormous importance.[15] To alleviate the pressure, Betsy decided to offer room and board, by way of the bedroom and sitting room, at 25 shillings a week to any summer season visitors. This somewhat inconvenienced both David and William as when there was a lodger they were whisked up to a shared attic room. The two boys were in the event thrilled to discover that one of these early summer tourist visitors was the barrister and novelist, Rider Haggard, the author of amongst other works, *King Solomon's Mines.* However, from Betsy's viewpoint, the extra few shillings of income garnered each week from this source were much appreciated.

David's own life accordingly reflected expanded horizons; his political thoughts, much influenced by injustices to the Welsh people, religion, social standing and landlordism, now extended to submitting articles to the local north Wales newspapers, hoping for publication, albeit under the pseudonym of 'Brutus'. The editor of the *North Wales Express*, instead of the expected rejection, asked for more engaging articles. No payment was of course forthcoming, but David was excited at the prospect of his published contributions. Later on, the *Caernarfon and Denbigh Herald* published David's essay on bits of poetry characterising local celebrities.[16] Underpinning this entry into journalism was his membership, from late 1881, sponsored by the local lay preacher, John Roberts, of the much famed Porthmadog Debating Society. His involvement was notable for his carefully crafted arguments and speeches. This was further expanded by his joining amateur dramatic groups in north Wales and more notably Cricieth's Debating Society. Later, whilst courting his future wife, Margaret Owen, David invariably invited her to the Debating Society meetings and lectures.[17] Again, whilst these endeavours created no income, they nevertheless served as confidence-building episodes in young David's life, effectively representing a campaign leading to his eventual first political success in 1890. Yet, still, he needed to maintain the pace of his solicitors' studies.

At the same moment, for ten days in late 1881, David set off for London (this gave him his first glimpse of the south of England) to face the terror of the Law Society's Intermediate Examination. A cousin (or possibly an uncle, husband of one of his father's four sisters), who fortunately lived in the capital, met him at Euston Station and accompanied him whilst he was there. He met this stern test with some apprehension, yet managed to secure a pass. In communicating this good news to Randall Casson, back in Cricieth, his principal's immediate reaction was to promptly congratulate David and suggest he took a week off to enjoy the sights of London, which David greatly appreciated. More to the point, Casson enclosed, with his warm greetings, a much valued postal order. Accordingly, an elated David took in all the sights including Covent Garden, Westminster Abbey and the Houses of Parliament, whose physical structure left a less than favourable impression on him as he noted in his diary: 'grand buildings outside, but inside they are crabbed, small and suffocating'.[18]

At the same time, his brother William now embarked on an identical legal career path and mother Betsy, as anticipated, needed to find yet another £180 indenture fee and stamp duty as thus, the second articled clerk was in the family, with Breese, Jones and Casson. For both brothers, admittedly at different levels, life was just study, study, study as the only, or near sole occupation.

Almost secretly, both David and William jointly entered into Cricieth's 'Castle Festival' essay competition that year, to pen a joint submission entitled 'Cash and Credit'. This secured, a little surprisingly, the first prize of two guineas, an undoubted boost to finances. David pondered on whether his uncle Richard Lloyd would have preferred the boys to spend more time preparing for their legal professional examinations, which for David were now scheduled to take place in early 1884. However David, of course, preferred involvement in Cricieth and Porthmadog local societies, which offered more prospects of regional fame and renown. David accordingly took the edge off his uncle's stern criticisms by agreeing to lead Sunday sermons on the evils of drunkenness. He even joined the United Kingdom Alliance (Blue Ribbon pledge of total liquor abstinence) in south Caernarfonshire, subsequently rising to the status of secretary. There are many accounts of David Lloyd George's temperance in this period and in particular, Roy Hattersley's *The Great Outsider*, pp.20-22 is most informative. Interestingly, David learned to enjoy a quiet drink with Randall Casson, even on a Sunday![19] Meanwhile, David pressed on with Randall Casson, learning more about everyday solicitors' business, and mercifully, by now, receiving minimal earnings. William undertook a similar process but, of course, his endeavours were unpaid. In summary, the George and Lloyd families, now with two legal apprentices to maintain, and less income available, found their home economy struggling, although income from lodgers did help a little. Almost embarrassingly, Richard Lloyd obtained 'loans' from family friends and acquaintances to avoid total hardship.

Betsy's reduced building society investment now came to end in disaster. Quite out of the blue, in late 1882, the news arrived that the Liverpool Building Society had collapsed, taking Betsy's capital with it. Serious poverty had now to be reckoned with. Luckily, the ever friendly William Williams, with thoughtful pastoral reasons, agreed to pay David's 1884 travel costs to London to take his solicitor examination finals, now delayed from January 1884 until the April. For good measure, another £1 was added 'towards family needs'.[20] W.R.P. George's account of the 'respectable poverty' ongoing in the early 1880s reads (from Richard Lloyd's diary of 1883 and 1884),

- 23 July 1883 – Paid back £2 borrowed from William Williams (WW) [from lodger income].
- 24 November 1883 – £1 loan from WW to pay D.Ll.G.'s Library Subscription.
- 9 January 1884 – Called at Ynysgain – Uncle [relative] still pretty poorly. He lent me £2, 10 shillings for my sister Betsy to buy flour.
- 4 February 1884 – Received 10 shillings from WW towards needs of our family.
- 12 April 1884 – Received £1 from WW to pay for slippers for D.Ll.G.[21]

When the results of David's 'finals' came through, after April 1884, to some extent uncle Richard Lloyd's concern about insufficient study being undertaken was justified. The result was that David had indeed passed but only achieved Third Class Honours. This was enough, however, to enable him to practise as a fully qualified solicitor. Randall Casson, upon hearing the news, immediately offered David the position of assistant solicitor with the firm's main office in Porthmadog with a salary of £1 a week, plus, which turned out to be a bone of contention, a commission on any new work introduced. Alternatively, he was offered the managing clerkship of the firm's affluent regional office in Dolgellau, about twenty-five miles distant. David believed he was being undervalued, no doubt weighing up what he might be able to earn as a solicitor in London, where of course he had recently visited. In the end, with little confidence at best, David accepted Casson's first offer at the Porthmadog office, although relations between the two, mainly owing to the commission aspect, brought bad grace into their working life. Plus, David would have been thinking of ongoing expenses to work by way of a rail season ticket, which apparently cost £3.[22]

Brother William, now himself nearing the end of his five-year articled period, tended to find himself as an unwilling go-between for his brother and Randall Casson, together with the fact that he, William, needed to proceed hopefully undisturbed towards his own next set of solicitors' examinations, scheduled for January 1885. As it happened, William also obtained a successful outcome, with First Class Honours at Intermediate level. Upon his return from the examinations in London, he quickly discovered that David had left Breese, Jones and Casson to set up his own business, operating from the back room of the family home at Morvin House. David had always made it clear that he wanted, above all, to 'get on'. One is left to speculate what the professional outcome might have been if Edward Breese, with his much wiser head, had not died so tragically in late 1880. After all, David was his personal protégé. So, David Lloyd George started his fully-fledged solicitor's life with a makeshift brass plate on the front door, but with no proper offices, no immediate clients and even without the £3 (this might take two or three successful cases to fund!) required to purchase the robe and neckband necessary for court appearances.[23] David's future was quite literally now in his own hands.

Indeed, it was a situation young David had envisaged a little earlier, as his diary entry of 2 June 1883 reveals. 'I believe it [my future] depends on what forces of pluck and *industry* I can muster'.[24] Yet, he recognised there were, nevertheless, some important aspects in his favour. John Grigg has selected these as David's breadth of local knowledge; an interesting level of contacts through Uncle Lloyd, and David's own ever-expanding experiences as an up and coming speaker. These recognisable talents and advantages went hand in hand with his ongoing understanding of Court procedure and magisterial ways. Grigg concludes, 'Between 1885 and 1890 it is virtually impossible to separate Lloyd George the solicitor from Lloyd George the politician'.[25]

However well-armed Lloyd George was with these indisputable personal attributes, the need to make a living was increasingly becoming the major priority. Unfortunately, Breese, Jones and Casson would never contemplate releasing the brilliantly competent brother William, still under articles, to Lloyd George's new business (that would come later) so Lloyd George's brain hatched an almost perfect alternative. Quite simply, Uncle Lloyd could act as receptionist-cum-clerk at the 'main office' at Morvin House, Cricieth, leaving Lloyd George to make his legal presence known well enough in the surrounding towns of Porthmadog, Ffestiniog (reportedly paying 3 shillings and 6 pence a week for rooms), and Pwllheli; in fact over the whole wider areas of Caernarfonshire and Merionethshire. He honed his undoubted skills in the lower courts up to County level, underpinned by his natural audacity (often to the surprise of magistrates), his quickness of mind and his clear attention to detail.[26]

Fees began to trickle in, gaining momentum due to Lloyd George's recognition and fame as a learned brief.[27] To these accolades must be added his paying heed to non-conformist opinion and positively involving himself in matters of the land, in particular the hugely unpopular tithe system. At one open-air meeting of the Anti-Tithe League, with Lloyd George attending in his capacity as a speaker, one churchman heckler was adequately stifled when Lloyd George's initial fee level as a practising solicitor, at 6 shillings and 8 pence, was challenged. In his response, Lloyd George implied that whereas the tithe payment was compulsory, going to see him in a professional capacity was not – it was a matter of choice.[28] By 1886, this interest in, if not obsession with, the land, expressed by his invaluable professional work, acting for those alleged to have offended landlords' interests in some way (such as poaching or trespass), set Lloyd George down the political road of land reform. In this context, he was now placing himself somewhere between Gladstonian retrenchment ideals, and Chamberlain's latest tax policy and land revision ideas. In the wake of the 1885 Parliamentary election results for the Liberal Party, he found an opportunity to enjoin a political meeting set up in February 1886 at Blaenau Ffestiniog, where the famed Irish Land League leader, Michael Davitt, was billed as the main speaker. Lloyd George recalls that he was 'very favourably impressed by his [Davitt's] presence'. Michael Davitt also, in return, by way of a compliment suggested Lloyd George might think of standing for Parliament.[29] There was even talk of Lloyd George's name being linked with potential future Parliamentary opportunities in both Caernarfonshire and Merionethshire, although reality quickly reared its head with the vital question of how the inevitable election expenses would be met.

Yet another more possible scheme now arose: newspaper involvement and better still, newspaper ownership itself. So, by late 1887, the Pwllheli-based *Utgorn Rhyddid (Trumpet of Freedom)* was launched by Lloyd George among others, and each contributing partner, it was proposed, was to contribute a maximum of £100 to the venture by way of an investment. David R. Daniel (the former secretary of the Ffestiniog Quarrymen's Union) was appointed editor; 'we want something stirring, never mind the bombast if the stuff is good', Lloyd George explained to Daniel.[30] Thus, as Lloyd George seriously began to forge his ambitions as a politician, he nevertheless had to take heed of the requirements of his ongoing professional business. The year 1887 saw his brother William pass his final Law Society examinations and thus could now freely join Lloyd George in partnership (not without some disappointment, verging on animosity, from Randall Casson), and by so doing, would ensure a better business base. Lloyd George recognised this, as his diary entry on 4 September 1887 reveals, 'I must attend to my business well, so as to build up a good practice [now William had joined him], practice economy so as to accumulate some measure of wealth; get all my cases well advertised and to subscribe [to local organisations] judiciously'. Almost automatically, he added, 'I must write political articles on Welsh politics so as to show my mastery of them'.[31]

Leaving aside his professional life and business opportunities, Lloyd George decided, after some years of semi-underhand courtship, to enter into the state of matrimony. His chosen lady was Margaret Owen, the only child of Richard and Mary Owen, of Mynydd Ednyfed farm. The farm itself was situated on the crest of a hill to the north of Cricieth. We need not concern ourselves, in this narrative, with the well documented period of courtship, from the church-sponsored outing to Bardsey Island in 1885 (some accounts prefer 1884). The vital question for Margaret's locally respected parents was the issue of David Lloyd George's financial status and means, together with his employment prospects. Only the best, they believed, for young Margaret. Thus, it would not do for Margaret to marry, as her parents saw it, beneath her. Richard Owen not only farmed, as a tenant, and leased 100 acres of land, he was very much practised in the art of stock valuations. He also had financial interests in the Porthmadog sailing fleet.[32] Moreover, he had sent Margaret to a private fee-paying school run by Dr. Williams in Dolgellau, some thirty miles distant from the farm. In short, Richard and Mary Owen were affluent, with two servants at the farm, and in a higher social class than either the Lloyds or the Georges. Local gossip had meant that the Owens harboured suspicions of Lloyd George's flirtatious history, and more especially, they were concerned over his reliability. What is more, the Owens were Methodists, and the Lloyd Georges were Campbellite Baptists! Using devious ways of communication, Lloyd George attempted to impress the Owens, not without success, although they still had suspicions over Margaret's husband to be. Perhaps they too were a touch angry, as indeed Margaret was, when Lloyd George undertook a 'breach of promise' legal case – pointing out that there was a good fee involved in this – involving a relative of a former lady friend of his. Margaret even wrote to Lloyd George strongly suggesting he should turn down the instructions.

More interesting, however, is the fact that Richard Owen made a new will on 27 May 1887, leaving his wife Mary a life interest in his estate and upon his demise, all assets would devolve to Margaret. One possible conclusion here is that Richard Owen was planning that David Lloyd George (or perhaps any other suitor for that matter) would never receive any of his estate, as everything must eventually be left to Margaret. Lloyd George would have been aware of this, as the will was drawn up by the new firm of Lloyd George and George, Solicitors, at Cricieth. Ffion Hague writes that, 'through the spring of

1887 and to that summer, Lloyd George continued to flirt [with other women]'; Margaret (now referred to by Lloyd George as Maggie) continued to upbraid him and Mrs. Owen continued with her disapproval.[33] As it so happened, towards the end of 1887, Maggie received three proposals of marriage from local influential suitors, but by this time, in spite of some remaining difficulties encountered with the Owens, Maggie and David decided to marry in early 1888. Breaking this news to their respective families presented a difficulty, as there were deeply held religious differences existing, and in particular, a decision needed to be made as to where the wedding ceremony would be held. Lloyd George needed to acquaint his family of the marriage plans although his own sister, Polly, was in confidence as Lloyd George outlined his likely immediate future fee earnings to her. Even Uncle Lloyd, kept in the dark until now, accepted the match and added, 'Everyone says that she is a lovely girl and a practical girl'.[34] Maggie, of course, was obliged to inform her parents of the decision, which she was now, being over twenty-one, able to dictate. Lloyd George (in late 1887) had already discussed his 'engagement with Maggie', in a not altogether friendly discussion, one evening at Mynydd Ednyfed, with Mr. and Mrs. Owen. Their advice was to wait to marry, essentially based upon their existing financial position. In conclusion, the meeting ended with the Owens asking Lloyd George to 'reconsider the matter and see them again [later] about the matter. Maggie was [separately] in the kitchen during the interview'.[35] Indeed, many thought highly of Maggie although some considered that she tended to be a little parsimonious, but overall, her excellent qualities shone through. The marriage took place at the religiously neutral Pencaenewydd Chapel, near Cricieth, on 24 January 1888, with very few witnesses. The happy couple left for honeymoon in London, which was only marred by a somewhat officious London cabman quarrelling with Lloyd George about the cost of the fare and no doubt his tip at Euston Station on the return journey back to Cricieth. David and Maggie Lloyd George now settled in to share the home of Mr. and Mrs. Owen at Mynydd Ednyfed, who had made part of the house ready for the newly married couple. They shared this home for three years.

The year 1888 would prove in many ways a pivotal point in the Lloyd Georges' lives, not least for David Lloyd George as he obtained, after some initial manoeuvring involving loyal colleagues, a virtually unassailable political prominence in the six-town Parliamentary constituency of Carnarvon Boroughs. The essential character of David Lloyd George was moulded in these early years and he now stood on the threshold of his political life.

Notes

1. Asquith's own boyhood and upbringing have striking, but not total, similarities.
2. Violet Bonham Carter, *An Intimate Portrait*, (Harcourt Brace New York, 1965), p.129, and David Carradine, *Aspects of Autocracy*, (Yale University Press, London, 1994), p.156.
3. J. Graham Jones interestingly refers to Welsh 'relative harmony and mutual respect between landlords and tenantry' in, *David Lloyd George and Welsh Liberalism*, (National Library of Wales, Aberystwyth 2010), p.4.
4. Roy Hattersley indicates the inheritance was £768 in, *David Lloyd George, the Great Outsider*, (Little Brown, London, 2010), p.6. Earlier, Peter Rowland states in *Lloyd George*, (Barrie and Jenkins, London, 1975), p.3, the net estate value as 'not exceeding £1,000', as did W.R.P. George, *The Making of Lloyd George*, (Faber & Faber, London, 1976), p.66. Most Lloyd George biographers agree on the income figure of £46.
5. Ffion Hague, *The Pain and the Privilege*, (Harper Collins, London, 2008), pp.16-37.
6. William George, *My Brother and I*, (Eyre and Spottiswoode, London, 1958), p.11.
7. Ffion Hague, *The Pain and the Privilege*, op. cit., pp.20-21.
8. William George, *My Brother and I*, op. cit., p.40.
9. Ibid., p.17.
10. Ibid., p.51.
11. Ibid., pp.107-109, received insurance money of 15 shillings, in March 1879.
12. W.R.P. George, *The Making of Lloyd George*, op. cit., p.84.
13. B.B. Gilbert, *David Lloyd George – A Political Life*, (Batsford, London, 1987), p.33.
14. William George, *My Brother and I*, op. cit., p.115.
15. William George refers to this period as being 'on the verge of respectable poverty'. Roy Hattersley, *The Great Outsider*, op. cit., p.20, and William George, *My Brother and I*, op. cit., p.108.
16. B.B. Gilbert, *David Lloyd George*, op. cit., p.44. Also, Richard Lloyd George, *My Father - Lloyd George*, (Crown, USA, 1961), p.29, reports, 'David's efforts were unpaid but highly relished'.
17. K. O. Morgan, *Lloyd George - Family Letters 1885-1936*, (Oxford University Press, Oxford, and University of Wales Press, Cardiff, 1973), p.15.

18. Peter Rowland, *Lloyd George*, (Barrie and Jenkins, London, 1975), p.33.
19. Martin Pugh, *Lloyd George*, (Longman, London, 1988), p.5. David spent 2 shillings and 6 pence, with a 1 shilling tip for the waitress, on refreshments when he was composing a speech, W.R.P. George, *The Making of Lloyd George*, op. cit., p.105. This, in itself suggests a reasonable level of spending income at the time.
20. Roy Hattersley, *The Great Outsider*, op. cit., p.25.
21. W.R.P. George, *The Making of Lloyd George*, op. cit., pp.116-117.
22. Roy Hattersley, *The Great Outsider*, op. cit., p.25
23. Frank Owen, *Tempestuous Journey*, (Hutchinson, London, 1954), p.42.
24. Herbert Du Parcq, *Life of David Lloyd George*, (Caxton Publishing, London 1912), Vol.1, p.42.
25. John Grigg, *The Young Lloyd George*, op. cit., p.45.
26. W. Watkin Davies, *Lloyd George*, (Constable, London, 1939), p.51.
27. Lloyd George himself writes (3 February 1886) 'Business pours in steadily'. Peter Rowland, *Lloyd George*, op. cit., p.51.
28. John Grigg, *The Young Lloyd George*, op. cit., p.50.
29. W.R.P. George, *The Making of Lloyd George*, op.cit., p.131.
30. Don M. Cregier, *Bounder from Wales* - Lloyd George's Career Before the First World War, (University of Missouri Press, Columbia, 1976), p.29.
31. K.O. Morgan (Ed.), *Lloyd George - Family Letters 1885-1936*, op. cit., pp.20-21.
32. This involved part-ownership, expressed in shares of 64 in total, of a merchant vessel.
33. Ffion Hague, *The Pain and the Privilege*, op. cit., p.85.
34. Ibid., p.92. See also William George, *My Brother and I*, op. cit., p.99, Maggie 'was a charming and sensible lassie'.
35. K.O. Morgan (Ed.) *Lloyd George - Family Letters 1885-1936*, op. cit., p.21.

2

1888-1904
The New Member of
Parliament, Gold and the Boers

'His oratory was forceful and sincere, yet factual and well organised'.
Donald McCormick, *The Mask of Merlin*[1]

Peter Rowland, in his study of Lloyd George, concurs that the year 1888 was a crucial time in the great man's life.[2] In the months after the wedding, three specific aspects arose, all of which, carrying into 1889 had, in one shape or another, financial implications. The first of these is colloquially known as the 'Llanfrothen burial case', the subject matter of which had been disturbing non-conformist minds for some years since 1881. Nevertheless, Lloyd George obtained considerable kudos in his role in this quite famous legal case. It is not beyond the realms of coincidence that Lloyd George managed to get himself appointed as the official solicitor to Cricieth's Burial Board. Following the Burials Act 1880, non-conformists had the right to be buried in (Church of England) Parish churchyards, according to their own religious rites. Anglican churchmen were not especially keen on this situation, but in this instance Lloyd George came up against an intransigent rector, the Rev. Richard Jones. After the death of a local quarryman, Robert Roberts, in 1888, Lloyd George, after receiving instructions from the family, thought he had found a way of getting around the rector's refusal to proceed with non-conformist rites, and suggested that the gates of the churchyard be broken into (as they were locked by the rector), and the family's preferred funeral proceeded with. The result of this was that the family was charged with trespass by the Rev. Jones, and Lloyd George proposed that the subsequent court case involve a jury. Lloyd George was well aware, no doubt from earlier courtroom clashes, that the appointed judge, John Bishop, was, as ever, bigoted, yet 'dreamy, slow and lacking in perspicacity'.[3] The case had all the ingredients of a drama and Lloyd George would play his role to the full. In essence, the case was heard, and the jury gave its verdict in favour of the Roberts family. After a two-month adjournment, Judge Bishop incorrectly announced the jury's findings and thus found favour with the wrong party in the dispute, and Lloyd George promptly proposed an appeal. as was the practice, this appeal was heard in London on 14 December 1888. The Lord Chief Justices upheld Lloyd George's appeal and equally admonished Judge Bishop. For Lloyd George, he had, single-handedly, struck a blow for Wales against the English-speaking establishment by way of an almost unbelievable stroke of luck. The law case itself was widely reported, especially throughout north Wales.[4]

The twenty-five-year-old lawyer, aside from greatly enhancing his legal prowess which would lead to more good fee-paying cases for Lloyd George and George, would additionally achieve another step towards securing a coveted Parliamentary constituency candidature nomination, hopefully for Caernarfon district. Already Lloyd George could bask in the Liberal successes in the first County Council elections of early 1889, and his acceptance of a nomination as an Alderman. Indeed, just ten days or so after these events, the Liberal Party in Carnarvon Boroughs proceeded to commence the selection procedure for their candidate, ready for the next General Election, expected in 1892. Naturally still glowing, from the Llanfrothen trial success, their choice would inevitably fall upon the current hero of the Welsh legal world, David Lloyd George. Hugh Edwards' 1913 description of Lloyd George was that he was in 1888, 'the coming man in Wales'. Lloyd George had to thank his friend, David Daniel, for his support and guidance. Daniel was, of course, Lloyd George's co-founder of the newspaper, *Utgorn Rhyddid* (1887). The smaller towns of Cricieth, Nefyn and Pwllheli quickly settled in favour of Lloyd George's nomination, followed later, after much deliberation,

21

by the towns of Conwy, Caernarfon and Bangor – the last initially being quite Tory and Anglican minded.

Maggie was increasingly worried, not just because she was expecting their first child – here was her new husband embarking upon a clear political course with no prospects of a salary. Her pleadings for a better financial base seemingly fell on deaf ears. How could they now live? Financially they were worse off than before the wedding. Could or would the ever-faithful William George solely shoulder the burdens of the new two-man solicitor's practice with one of the two brother partners effectively only having a part-time involvement? The Lloyd Georges' first born, Richard, duly arrived on 15 February 1889, creating more pressure for Lloyd George to concentrate on the question of income.

The second great issue of the year now reared its head, much to the consternation of local politicians. Lloyd George's virtual web of localised social contacts had already extended to Cricieth's Amateur Dramatic Society 'where the company was congenial and he could indulge in his love of oratory'.[5] Amongst the ever present budding thespians was a handsome widow of some wealth (and indeed a Liberal activist) Mrs. J(ones). We have no need here to dwell on the inevitable suspicions that fellow actor to be, Lloyd George, was responsible for this lady's state of impending motherhood. The rumours reached the ever straining ears of the constituency's Liberal Association – and that would not do. Equally great endeavours were made to make sure Maggie did not find out. Lloyd George's more modern biographers tell this tale, or at least allude to his paternity. Earlier writers, such as du Parcq and Hugh Edwards, would fail to mention this threat. However, Richard Lloyd George's 1961 book puts it more succinctly, 'this particular affair with Mrs. J. was in the category of a spontaneous overflow of his [father's] prodigious energies'.[6] Fortunately for Lloyd George, Mrs. J. proved a compliant and helpful individual and with William George's skills cunningly in play, the whole affair was covered up, all underpinned by the purchase of 'an annuity [being] obtained for the lady at considerable cost'. She had to sign a solemn covenant that nothing about the relationship should ever be divulged and that the forthcoming child would never be photographed, nor indeed the father acknowledged – otherwise 'the annuity would be forfeited for ever'.[7] In Olwen Carey-Evans' (née Lloyd George) own book of 1985, she writes, 'even before my brother Dick was born there was a scandal surrounding Father and another woman and the family tacitly accepted that the son born to Mrs. J. was our half brother'.[8] Olwen herself can be described as sensible and level headed and we have every reason to accept her words. The annuity settlement was speedily organised and put in place. Maggie never heard of these rumours at the time. Nevertheless some practical questions remain. Where were the necessary monies to acquire such an annuity to come from? It is virtually impossible to imagine Lloyd George, even with or without his brother's help, finding the necessary purchase price. Was the firm of Lloyd George and George prosperous enough to pay for this or borrow some capital to fund the purchase? Bentley Brinkerhoff Gilbert provides the most likely answer in his description of David Lloyd George's political life. Lloyd George's 'career was saved when Liberal supporters bought her [Mrs. Jones] off, with an annuity – this may have occurred'.[9]

Secondly, what sort of annuity was this? In twentieth- and twenty-first-century insurance jargon any annuity is a guaranteed series of annual payments for the purchaser's lifetime not dependent upon any other underlying conditions. One is led to speculate that 'however funded' Lloyd George and George's business bought a right to income for life, worded in some way or another (and no doubt earning some introductory commission from the life insurance office on the purchase price), and channelled income payments through to Mrs. J(ones) once she had signed the covenant of silence. Such a purchase would cause a high financial burden on the business and undoubtedly create an overdraft position at the bank (see later). In that practical way, payments could come in via the solicitors' business, and if the agreement was ever transgressed, be equally annulled at any time by the partners. Thus, on this scenario, the technical term annuity could well be a misnomer.

Quite unaware of her husband's alleged infidelity, Maggie's life at Mynydd Ednyfed inevitably revolved around the recently born Richard (Dick), and she soon found herself expecting another child. Lloyd George's life as a solicitor and politician, with his ever increasing round of social speaking engagements, were in another world. On 20 March 1890, however, they were planning to go by train to Caernarfon for a day's relaxation. Whilst at the railway station what was to be, effectively, a life changing telegram, arrived addressed to Lloyd George. Maggie herself read the message, 'Swetenham died last night'. Edward Swetenham was the sitting Conservative member for Carnarvon Boroughs and he had died of a sudden heart attack, thereby creating a need for a Parliamentary by-election. Her husband, David Lloyd George, already had the Liberal nomination and the Conservatives chose as their representative in the forthcoming contest the Llanystumdwy Squire, Hugh Ellis-Nanney. So it was to be the Welsh speaking, locally based man, against the politically experienced yet non-Welsh speaking landowning member of the gentry. William George's diary entry for Easter Monday, 7 April 1890 reads, 'The struggle is not so much a struggle of Tory versus Liberal or Radical even; the main issue is between a country squire and an upstart Democrat'.[10] Lloyd George, his brother William and Uncle Lloyd threw themselves wholesale into the impending campaign, of which Lloyd George's main electoral appeal to the 4,366 registered voters in the constituency was based on the twin political themes of religious liberty and equality for Wales. J. Graham Jones explains that this 'rising tide of political opinion championed by Tom Ellis, Lloyd George and young zealots of Cymru Fydd, emphasised the economic exploitation of the Welsh tenant farmers as well as religious discrimination and political intimidation, and thus demanded specific economic remedies'.[11] On 10 April 1890, the polls opened, and the votes were counted the very next day. On a near 90 per cent turnout, Lloyd George, after two recounts, secured 50.2 per cent of the votes cast, with Ellis-Nanney achieving a very close 49.8 per cent – they were only separated by eighteen votes.[12] Lloyd George summarised his success, 'the day of the cottage bred man has at last dawned'.[13] The road to Westminster now lay ahead. David and Maggie's lives were, in different ways, now changed, for ever. Lloyd George's Parliamentary dream had now arrived, yet Maggie wept, seeing her expectations of marriage to a country solicitor now evaporate. And yet, two stumbling blocks remained. How were the election expenses themselves to be paid for, and more immediately, how could Maggie and Lloyd George manage on his new unsalaried position as a Member of Parliament (and thus with no proper time to further build up his professional solicitor's business) – equally, how did this leave the family in general? Undoubtedly, as regards the latter, William George would not necessarily have foreseen the practicalities which would mean he might not be able to provide an ongoing salary for himself and his brother, an economic struggle that effectively persisted until 1905. To his credit, Lloyd George was not unaware of the manifestly unjust reality of this.

As to the 1890 election expenses, of £200, which were beyond doubt an obstacle for Lloyd George, these were, happily, covered when 'a committee of [local] Liberals and several Bangor and Caernarfon lawyers offered [Lloyd George] their services as election agents without charge'.[14] In fact, the main bulk of the £200 came from a wealthy local Methodist Liberal supporter who initially demurred from contributing due to Lloyd George's youthful appearance. After hearing him speak, the Lloyd George charm won the day, and the promised £200 was secured. Reference to the North Wales Liberal Federation Records (unavailable) could well give more detail.

Lloyd George set out for London on 16 April 1890, as the youngest Member of Parliament (MP) in the House of Commons. He was met at Euston Station by Alfred Davies, a wealthy Welshman living in London; his election agent, J.T. Roberts, travelled with him.[15] The new member was formally introduced to the Speaker of the House by Arthur Acland (Radical MP for Rotherham) and Stuart Rendel (MP for Montgomeryshire) who each had links with Wales and interest in Welsh issues in general. In Parliament he was joined by other Welsh Liberals or Radicals, namely Herbert Lewis, Frank Edwards, Samuel Evans and D.A. Thomas. Lloyd George wisely decided to sit quietly, study the Commons procedures and rules, and above all, listen. Nevertheless, he was less quiet outside the Commons chamber. His countrywide speeches were always received with rapture; his oratorical reputation preceded him.

Back in Cricieth, Mr. and Mrs. Richard Owen had decided to retire and they were busy realising assets, accordingly. With this liquidity, Richard Owen arranged for the building of a pair of tall, semi-detached houses, overlooking Cricieth's bay. One of these was for himself and his wife Mary, and the other, named Brynawelon, very kindly set aside for use by Maggie, Lloyd George and the children, Richard, and Mair, born 2 August 1890. Meanwhile, Lloyd George's daily Parliamentary work entailed a stable London base to supersede the temporary residential options of lodging with the Welsh Davies family in Acton, or with other friends, and on occasions staying at the National Liberal Club. In early 1891, he took on lease a set of rooms in Verulam Buildings, Grays Inn, at a yearly cost of £70. This included a porter at the gate and two housekeepers on the premises. Maggie joined him there until May 1891, and later for a few weeks in June and July, although not at all thereafter until the lease was assigned at the end of the 1892 Parliamentary session.[16] Earlier, on 13 June 1890, Lloyd George took the opportunity of undertaking his Commons maiden speech on the compensation terms contained in the Local Taxation Bill. Lloyd George specifically endorsed the Welsh Members' general proposal that any Welsh money so available should be directed to Welsh educational requirements. After the bishops, the brewers were his next favourite target this time. All went well enough with his good humoured contribution and even William Ewart Gladstone was reported to be exceedingly delighted, as were, to a lesser extent, A.J. Balfour, Joseph Chamberlain and Sir William Harcourt. The press gave excellent reviews; the *Daily Graphic* rated his endeavours as 'rather clever', *The Pall Mall Gazette* exclaimed Lloyd George's efforts as 'capital', and his speech was mentioned in *The Times*' leading article.[17] Lloyd George himself writes in his diary, 14 June 1890, 'There was no doubt I scored a success and a great one ... several members congratulated 'Wales' upon my speech'.[18] A few days earlier, Lloyd George had dined with Stuart Rendel (1834-1913), who became a lifelong friend, with Gladstone also being present. Lloyd George greatly appreciated Rendel's friendship. Rendel himself had made his fortune in connection with Armstrongs in the north of England, a munitions supplier. Moreover, Rendel was related to Gladstone by marriage.[19]

Privately, Lloyd George still had money worries. The solicitors' Welsh base provided (the business premises had now moved to Porthmadog), courtesy of brother William, some cash drawings and, as time went by, some income did arise from the London base of the newly formed Lloyd George & Co. solicitors practice. Newspaper articles and other journalistic work continued to produce fees, but making financial ends meet was by far and away the main ongoing challenge. Indeed, the shortage of money dogged his very existence. At this time, William George received a letter from Lloyd George, 'I haven't got any cash, will you bring me £10 with you tomorrow without fail, or I shall be in the dickens of a pickle'.[20] W.R.P. George tells of Lloyd George's next cash raising scheme, which involved getting Samuel Storey, the affluent Liberal MP for Sunderland, interested in providing most of the money required to buy out the newspapers in Caernarfon. Additionally, the idea was to obtain legal work for the solicitors practice with this venture and to benefit from the ownership of a much desired friendly press in north Wales. The newspaper proprietors wished to be assured of a cash transaction, which was set at £11,000 for both the *Genedl* and the *Herald.* Lloyd George's intention was to purchase the business promptly, re-equip same with new printing machinery, and then sell for a profit, the suggested total proceeds being £15,000. Obviously, the financial gain meant more than the continuance of a favourable press outlet. Lloyd George adds, 'This transaction ought to pay – I shall charge professionally, in any event'. William George showed no interest, evidently regarding it as one of his brother's pipe dreams.[21] However, one fruitful and increasing, albeit small, source of income was now being achieved to supplement Lloyd George's drawings from the Porthmadog solicitors practice offices. He writes to William George on 30 June 1891, on the subject of remunerative newspaper article earnings; 'if they [*The Star*] left a few lines out which should have brought it [his article] to half a column, I shall get 15 shillings instead of a guinea'. If they pay at the usual rate of £1 10 shillings per half column, I shall do well. This week [thus] between the *Manchester Guardian*, *The Star* and *Genedl*, I shall earn 6 guineas'.[22]

In the House of Commons, Lloyd George's confidence grew remarkably swiftly, with his quick and searching mind easily bent to the question of Welsh Church disestablishment, aspects of quarry royalties, railway rates and the much vexed Welsh tithe question. On occasions, this was without the immediate support of his fellow Welsh Members. Then the 1892 General Election came; more expense. Fortunately, the Carnarvon Boroughs constituency funds covered some of the cost, and local members additionally provided financial support for the cost of speech making journeys, other electoral gatherings, and hospitality. Even so, Lloyd George's campaign from late June 1892 was run sparingly, with just over £338 being personally spent. Thus, it worked out that the Liberals spent

3/6d to secure each Liberal vote! The Conservative equivalent was 5/1d.[23] According to his personal bank account details (the account was held with The National Bank of Wales, Caernarfon Branch) he had a month before polling day a £45 credit balance, although by the date of the poll count, a few weeks later, this had been replaced by an overdrawn figure of £123. Outstanding costs had also to be settled for printing the 35,000 election leaflets, and there were other local agents' costs. Fortunately, the Welsh National Council of the Disestablishment Committee made a £100 grant towards overall election expenditure. After all these costs had been accounted for by mid-August 1892, the personal overdraft had increased to £220. Regrettably, Lloyd George incurred the displeasure of Beriah Evans, the managing editor for the printers, for suggesting some overcharging had occurred, when in reality, Evans had organised a discount on the printing composition costs and the value of the paper supplied. Evans wrote to Lloyd George's new agent, R.O. Roberts, registering his disappointment at this allegation, describing same as 'ungenerous on your part and I presume also on Mr. Lloyd George's'. Interestingly, Watkin Davies, in his book, *Lloyd George*, claims that Lloyd George 'had rejected the offer of his admirers in the Carnarvon Boroughs to defray his election expenses'.[24]

At the count, Lloyd George had substantially increased his earlier majority – this time over the Tory challenger, the respected Sir John Puleston, then Constable of Caernarfon Castle – to 196 votes. Since the 1890 Parliamentary contest, Lloyd George had fallen out with his election agent, J.T. Roberts. Lloyd George's diary entry of 10 May 1892 refers to being 'very anxious to get rid of him' and asserts that Roberts was 'constantly bickering and quarrelling with me at every opportunity ... so I am gladly going to accept his resignation'. As has been seen, he was swiftly replaced by Mr. R.O. Roberts, a Caernarfon solicitor.[25] The prosperous Welsh society in London now gave an even greater welcome to Lloyd George, not always necessarily to his liking. The drapery business of D.H. Evans offered him a directorship of 300 guineas a year, plus 500 shares; which was declined by Lloyd George as he felt he would effectively be reduced to the role of a 'guinea pig' if accepted.[26] He was initially attracted to D.H. Evans' successful business in London, his fine house in Regents Park showing off the numerous Royal Academy paintings held there, all pointing to a large fortune. However, Lloyd George described Evans as 'light headed and feather brained' and, somewhat unusually, took an instant dislike to his wife, describing her as 'purse proud and consequently contemptible'.[27] These personal feelings in all probability were the main reason for his refusal of the business proposition. Nevertheless, welcome as it was whilst his Constituency Association (plus extra subscriptions from the more well-heeled members in Caernarfon) financed his basic Parliamentary expenses plus costs at election time, the matter of meeting daily personal outgoings was paramount. His family was expanding, another daughter, Olwen, was born on 3 April 1892 in Cricieth.

In the financial year 1893-1894, his gross income, from all sources, was £338 (which included £57 from the *Manchester Guardian*) and income tax on this total income figure amounted to over £6. Also, he had to cover the cost of running two homes and feeding and clothing all the family.[28] In the hope of saving some domestic costs, the lease on Verulam Buildings was given up and Lloyd George again lodged temporarily with the Davies family in Acton, London, and later went back to the National Liberal Club. He then leased rooms at Essex Court, in the Temple, from Tom Ellis at £25 per year in 1892 (Maggie only visited occasionally, otherwise she much preferred Cricieth), and the next year, 1893, he found a more permanent London base at Palace Mansions, Addison Road, Kensington, at an annual rent of £90.[29] Lloyd George began to ponder where, as curtailing expenditure was difficult, he could make some money and make it quickly; no doubt prompted by a letter from a business bank manager in Cricieth reporting an overdraft of £1,583. One immediate scheme came to mind.

As is well known, Lloyd George despised inherited privilege and the blessings associated with property and landownership. Yet as already observed, self-made men in general did appeal to his sense of admiration. He was, potentially, liable to be over-awed by financially successful individuals who had made their own fortune, and the suggestion that he could make a quick profit on shares in an Argentine gold mine stimulated huge interest. Earlier, in the 1860s, people from throughout Wales had emigrated to Patagonia in South America to enjoy a better life in a new Welsh-speaking colony and escape the growing Anglicisation in Wales, with the added potential of income from gold mining. On hearing of this, Lloyd George's interest in the Welsh Patagonian Gold Field Syndicate (registered offices at Effingham House, Arundel Street, Strand, London), which dated from late 1892 until early 1893, rocketed. The venture now took up most of his time and he managed to get the solicitors business, Lloyd George & Co., nominated as legal advisers to the syndicate. For himself, Lloyd George could take a 10 per cent commission on share transactions, plus fees of five guineas to attend each directors' meeting in London with the rank of deputy chairman. Lloyd George outlined his participation requirements, at this stage, by way of his diary entry on 7 January 1893, 'At this very moment I am supposed to be discussing the question of issuing debentures in order to raise money'.[30] To a large extent this venture, with insufficient research as regards the technical knowledge of gold actually being there, can be described best as 'improbable speculation'. With his financial brief before him, Lloyd George enthusiastically went about the business of obtaining venture capital by selling shares to would-be and eager investors. Major E.R. Jones, Liberal MP for Caernarfon and a successful publisher (the Effingham House address, above, was appropriate for his business), and Dr. G.B. Clarke, MP for Caithness, Scotland, willingly joined the group, as did R.O. Davies of Acton, Alfred Thomas, MP for East Glamorgan and, more reluctantly David's brother, William, and his cousin William Jones of Cae'r Dyni. At the end of 1892, after all the shares had been allocated and Lloyd George had received his share dealing commissions, it was decided to send a mining engineer, a Harlech man who held the original mineral rights, a Mr. David Richards, to 'assess the potential value of the operation'. Bentley Brinkerhoff Gilbert, in his book *David Lloyd George*, also referred to 'Captain' Richards, in Lloyd George's letters to his wife. In letter 293 (15 November 1892) Lloyd George referred to a third party view, 'Gully had a good opinion of Richards', whilst, in letter 296 (1 December 1892) Lloyd George described Richards as 'unreliable'. Shortly later in Letter 315 (4 January 1893), Lloyd George writes to his wife, concluding, conversely, that 'Richards had made a careful and close observation of the whole thing, and knew what this was about'.[31] After receiving Richards' disparaging reports of gold potential, a second expert, Von Heking, was despatched to the gold fields, followed by a third mining engineer, Hoefer. He somewhat rubbished Richards' report of little viability with claims of 'the gold deposits are no doubt exceedingly rich', but went on to condemn the project to failure because it 'lacked capital and competent management',[32] neither conclusion dwelling on whether the gold was actually there.

William George, once informed of the likelihood of a pessimistic outcome, customarily retorted with some far sightedness, 'What if the gold mine turns out to be a mere illusion of the Patagonian desert?'[33] At this point, William George could have advised caution or better still urged his brother to withdraw, but no, Lloyd George then went on to another gold mining cash share-raising endeavour, although he privately advised Maggie of the fiasco reached to date. So, by late 1892, the whole £5,000 share issue had been taken up, including new contributions from a successful chemist, J.T. Hughes, Thomas Lewis, a prosperous flour merchant and late Liberal MP for Anglesey, and W.J. Parry, former Chairman of Caernarfon County Council.[34] With this new found cash, the syndicate company's position, despite the basic concept of no gold being located, took on a better appearance. By March 1893, Parry, now promoted to the status of general manager, was despatched, with David Richards in attendance, to Argentina, to 'investigate and examine'. He would be paid £450 plus 200 shares in the syndicate for his trouble. Lloyd George independently recruited Hoefer, already in Patagonia, to report on Richard and Parry.[35] Roy Hattersley writes that, 'Had Uncle Lloyd been aware of the entire enterprise, 'so near to being a fraud perpetrated on gullible investors', he would have been horrified'.[36] Lloyd George writes, 'Patagonia is, I fear, a failure ... Hoefer wires that the property falls short of representations ... Don't let Uncle or anyone else know'.[37] Certainly, by late March 1894, Uncle did know! Grigg reports that Uncle Lloyd 'now has 10 shares and Margaret Lloyd George 15 ... [brother] William's holding is unchanged at 600' – equally William clearly (in due course) wished to distance himself from the fiasco, as he makes no mention at all of these arrangements and indeed none about the syndicate, in his own book, *My Brother and I*.[38] Even Lloyd George's appetite for instant profit quietly lapsed. Hopes for new investors failed, arguments about expenses at the mine continued, Richards and Parry's reports contradicted, and, of course, no gold was discovered. By late November 1894, the syndicate, for all intents and purposes, was wound up, with significant investor losses.

31

Including its legal entity, the syndicate was virtually extinguished by 6 December 1900.[39] Even as late as early November 1906, Lloyd George was still scheming and dreaming of success, and if further investor monies were to materialise, Lloyd George and William George would then have a total shareholding between them of 4,570 shares – alas it came to nothing.[40]

The entire episode places substantial doubt on Lloyd George's financial scruples and no less so on his poor judgment of others' financial backgrounds and alleged money experiences. Indeed, in late August 1986 Lloyd George undertook a later tour of Argentina with Herbert Lewis, in the guise of a holiday. lasting until that October, the expedition conceivably included some first- and second-hand investigations and site inspections of the Patagonian 'gold mine' areas. Even so, Lloyd George, with every good reason, essentially kept silent about the entire Patagonian episode. John Grigg, however, has carefully unearthed the underlying detail to the full. Prof. K.O. Morgan's summary explains 'while many shareholders found their investment to be worthless, the firm of Lloyd George and George was more than adequately rewarded for its legal assistance and advice'.[41]

By the end of December 1894, the month in which a fourth child, Gwilym, was born, Lloyd George demonstrated a fresh level of sensible financial acumen; he took out a life insurance policy (£500 cover, payable on death) with the Northern Assurance Company, at an annual premium of £34. 16 shillings – at least it gave some measure of real protection to his family.[42]

Lloyd George lost his mother, the beloved Betsy, on 19 June 1896. He was aware of the immense debt he owed to her and he returned to Cricieth for the funeral on 23 June, although few others attended. Maggie was ill at the time and stayed at home. As far as Lloyd George's personal and financial aspects were concerned, he now decided to live again, temporarily, at the National Liberal Club during 1894 and 1895, followed in 1897 by rooms at the Bingham Hotel in Chancery Lane, London. From 1899 until 1904, Margaret lived with Lloyd George at 179 Trinity Road, Wandsworth Common although she, much more than he, retreated to Brynawelon in Cricieth from time to time. There they remained until 1904, just prior to Lloyd George's Cabinet appointment.[43] Indeed, these last few years of the nineteenth century also saw the deaths of George Osborne Morgan

(1897), Thomas Gee (1898), and Tom Ellis (1899), all political contemporaries of Lloyd George.

Politics, or at least Welsh considerations, dominated very much throughout the 1890s. Disestablishment and disendowment of the dominant English Church had been his first priority, or at least this is what he portrayed to the electorate, but this was not necessarily the main interest of the Liberal Party as a whole. After Gladstone's retirement from the House of Commons in 1894, Welsh Liberal MPs included Lloyd George in their pressure group for assurances on the importance of Welsh issues, firstly with Harcourt and later with Rosebery who, on the surface, gave some support. Lloyd George, always firstly his own man and secondly for the Liberal Party, consequently lost some Parliamentary support, even being blamed for the Liberals' poor electoral showing in 1895. Even his efforts to negotiate the merger or some other lower level of amalgamation between the North and South Wales Liberal Associations came to nothing. His own Parliamentary majority in the General Election of 1895, against his old foe Squire Nanney, was only two votes higher than in 1892 despite there being a slightly larger number of electors on the register in a seat always regarded as a marginal.[44] Yet again Caernarvon Boroughs Liberal Association fought the General Election campaign with acute money difficulties. Mr. R.D. Williams, secretary to both the Carnarvon Boroughs and adjoining Arfon Constituencies, wrote to Lloyd George on 29 May 1895, complaining of his workload, his lack of campaign money, plus the interesting remark that Williams himself had not been paid his due salary for over twelve months. Williams also pressed the point about the outstanding investigatory work still needed on the constituency voters' register. He was particularly worried about the better organised Tories stealing a march on the Liberals here. After the announcement of his successful re-election, Lloyd George promptly left for Radnorshire to assist fellow radical, Frank Edwards (who lost by 79 votes). The 1895 election had totally exhausted Lloyd George and had actually rendered him temporarily deaf in addition. He rested for part of August at Cricieth, and then left for Oban in Scotland on 7 September with the Davies family of Acton, until 24 September. There were suspicions that the affluent Mr. and Mrs. Davies footed the bill.[45]

Nevertheless, he continued to expound, as and when he could, Welsh interests in Parliament. Equally, Lloyd George pursued one of his favoured personal interests, namely foreign travel, to Rome, South America, Switzerland, Paris, Italy, Canada, Austria and Portugal, mostly with friends and colleagues, yet only rarely with Maggie. Her first preference was, of course, always for north Wales. The question therefore needs to be asked how each of these foreign trips was funded, bearing in mind that no ordinary (non-ministerial) Member of Parliament was paid at this time, and Lloyd George's professional income, however achieved, was his sole means of support. Some comparison with Churchill is relevant here, as during his life Churchill earned more money from writing than from the political arena; although his opulent, wasteful lifestyle hardly helped. Nevertheless, Churchill was paid £250 per month for his journalist reports during the Boer War and in 1903 was commissioned to write the life of his father, for which he was given the staggering payment of £8,000.[46] Lloyd George was fortunate that friends, colleagues and successful Welsh businessmen stepped in and provided the necessary funding.

Interestingly, on a later occasion, when Lloyd George and his brother left for Italy in 1905, Mrs. 'Tim' Davies was there to wave goodbye – a moment not forgiven by Maggie.[47] Mrs. Davies remained a thorn in the flesh for Margaret. After a flurry of acrimonious correspondence between Lloyd George and Maggie, the latter acquiesced to the view that no scandalous sexual affair had arisen between her husband and Mrs. Davies. The eldest child, Richard Lloyd George, observed the situation as a youngster, and remembered Mrs. Davies as a 'lively, attractive creature, rather loquacious, very stylish and perhaps a little flamboyant' individual and regarded her husband Mr. Davies as a 'colourless personality ... [having] little real talent or distinction'.[48] Apparently, one of Mrs. Davies' own friends believed one of the Davies children had been fathered by Lloyd George. Hot on the heels of that disruption came the Kitty Edwards affair, again Lloyd George being accused of fathering her child. This instance was confined, effectively, to north Wales, and, legally, after a court case, Lloyd George emerged innocent and damages paid. C.P. Scott, editor of the *Manchester Guardian*, rallied to support Lloyd George and at a later time was heard to remark 'in [my] opinion, Dafydd [Lloyd

George] was not a lover of money(!)' and such a declaration went a long way to appease any public concerns. He also separately urged Lloyd George, in a letter dated 8 October 1903, 'Balfour must be fought and fought seriously'.[49] Interestingly, Lloyd George's London solicitors practice, now with a new partner, Arthur Rhys Roberts, (a Newport solicitor) operated from the new London business premises at 13 Walbrook, London, EC1, and dealt with the case in conjunction with William George in Wales.

Economies in the two Lloyd George households, Criccieth and London, were effectively exhausted. Lloyd George writes to Maggie in 1897, both complaining and offering a solution, 'I draw far more than my share of the [solicitors business] profits though I don't attend to one tenth of the work, this is neither fair nor honourable, and I feel sure you do not wish it to continue'. He proceeds to blame the cost of running two homes; dismisses as impractical combining a full political and equally full professional life undertaken at the same time. Lloyd George suggests a compromise by not living in London, particularly as Maggie detests city life, but 'if you prefer we can take a home in the suburbs – say Ealing or Acton ... the area is quite as good as anything you can get in Wales as it is free from smoke ... or if you prefer we can go further out and live, say, in Brighton'.[50] This suggestion of less expenditure came to nothing, although Maggie came to London to live with her husband in 1898, leaving Brynawelon in Criccieth let, and Lloyd George furthered his interests in southern England, especially the county of Sussex.

It was during the late 1890s that Lloyd George developed his lifelong interest in the game of golf, undoubtedly originating from his previous Scottish holiday. He writes to his brother William, extolling the virtues of the game and in the letter refers to Maggie by the now occasionally preferred pet name of Beggan. He writes, '[Maggie] was much more proficient in the use of golf sticks than Mrs. D[avies]. Now that we have links at Criccieth, we must get up a club. It provides fine exercise ... men and women alike take to it. The equipment is just a little expensive at first but they last a lifetime ... 30 shillings fixes you up [in clubs, etc.] as a golfer for the rest of your natural life'.[51] Clearly, club membership at the new local seaside links course at Criccieth, from 1895, would follow, as would membership of the Lewes Golf Club, near Brighton in Sussex. Lloyd George played at Lewes in the late 1890s with notable personalities such as Tim Davies, Edwin Cornwell, Thomas James Macnamara, Thomas Artemus Jones and Henry Massingham, all either politicians or newspaper men. Lloyd George was eventually elected a member of the Lewes Golf Club in 1902, with a two guinea membership charge. He immediately fell foul of the Lewes club secretary for employing unauthorised caddies. Thereafter, his name disappears from club membership records. However, he also became a member of the Royal Mid-Surrey Golf Club.[52]

From 1897, Lloyd George worked in the new London solicitors venture, whose offices in Walbrook, EC1, then moved to 63 Queen Victoria Street, hoping to generate more disposable income. Lloyd George estimated the likely annual running costs of this new London office to be about £600, including £200 as Roberts' salary. Clearly there would be, at least initially, a further call on the Porthmadog office of Lloyd George and George for yet more financial support and subsidy. In July 1898, Lloyd George writes to William indicating that the London office income could well amount to £295 plus a further £200 by that year end.[53] After a few years, this professional business became moderately prosperous (although during the Boer War period, less so). However, it did mean eventually less pressure on the ever faithful William George, labouring for the Cricieth and Porthmadog practices. The final quarter of 1899 saw Lloyd George and George of Cricieth debit net drawings of £276 12 shillings and 1 penny to Lloyd George, clearly to cover the Cricieth household expenses, the rent paid to his father-in-law and the two quarters' rent (£45) on the London base at Addison Road, Kensington.[54] Again, the business bank manager in Cricieth warned of an ongoing overdraft situation, after taking the Christmas holiday costs out of that business bank account. Journalistic fees, as has been seen, (*The Star* and the *Manchester Guardian*) coming in regularly did give some measure of relief. Yet the disaster in Argentina failed to prevent Lloyd George from embarking on another 'get rich quick' scheme. A simple and easy financial windfall was all that he needed, and then at least he might be able to keep up, financially, with his Parliamentary colleagues. In the summer of 1897, Lloyd George felt such an opportunity for swift, rich pickings had surfaced. He had already crossed swords with the slate mining Lord Penrhyn that year, in support of the striking workers at the slate quarries, and yet he would not be deterred in an endeavour to buy a slate mine for himself. Once more, a speculative project loomed large in his mind; acquisition of the Dorothea slate quarry in Nantlle Valley, Caernarfonshire. By necessity, such a purchase would involve finding financial backing, plus some likely high fees for his London solicitors' practice. The quarry purchase price was £160,000 and, eager as ever, Lloyd George thought he had persuaded Walter Owen Clough (Liberal, Portsmouth) and Adolphus Druckner (Tory, Northampton) to find the money, and failing that, a wealthy 'influential gentleman from Yorkshire'; who later withdrew. Further attempts to raise money came to nothing, despite a cash and share offer. Margaret clearly had misgivings, and Lloyd George comments 'I am sorry to say the whole affair upon which we have built so many hopes must [did] fall through'[55] – no more Dorothea.

More enthusiasm appeared for the next speculative hope, obtaining a directorship in a large Manchester-based insurance company, and this ran on to 1899, only to disappear from his life, equally swiftly. He needed to raise £60,000 but could only, with others, muster £41,000 – this figure included directors' guarantees. Such a company, once formed, could then purchase a newspaper such as the *Daily News*.[56]

As the nineteenth century came to a close, the political agenda in the House of Commons, or at least that of the Liberals in opposition, tended to be bogged down with arguments about the 1896 Education Bill, and the more vexed and ongoing question of Irish Home Rule. As has been seen, Lloyd George's interest often lay elsewhere. His appetite was whetted with Lord Penrhyn and the ongoing 1897 slate quarry workers' dispute, and now stretched forward to his special *bête noir*, the abolition, or at least substantial power reduction of the House of Lords. Lloyd George was horrified to discover that Lord Penrhyn's profits in 1898 from slate mining activities alone amounted to £133,000, yet his record of expenditure on safety measures for the poorly paid slate miners was abysmal. Any issue that aided the poor at the expense of greedy landlords or the aristocracy was of immense appeal.[57] In May 1899, Lloyd George was invited to join the House of Commons Select Committee, chaired by Henry Chaplin, the Member for Sleaford, and the terms of reference included the retirement pension funded by direct taxation. Figures were bandied about in the committee and eventually the chairman accepted Lloyd George's eager suggestion that 5 shillings a week would be the minimum national retirement pension (eventually, nearly ten years later, payable from age seventy). These proposals ensured a Conservative government would defer implementation on the grounds of expenditure and, as a delaying tactic, Conservative ministers set up a separate committee of enquiry to examine the costs and administration aspects. Anything that might also discomfort the Conservative and Unionist parties was grist to Lloyd George's mill. Nevertheless, the credit for the original idea of State-funded retirement pensions belongs to the Conservative Joseph Chamberlain, who looked into this in the 1880s. It was left for the 1906-1910 Liberal administration to actually introduce the Old Age Pension scheme on 9 January 1908.

Separately, Lloyd George was included in the mid-1899 House of Commons delegation to Canada. The High Commissioner, Lord Strathcona, paid for some members of the British House of Commons to come to North America to study and advise on the conditions for those Welshmen who wished to emigrate to the New World and what the motivation was behind such ideas. Lloyd George sailed on the S.S. *Bavarien* on 19 August 1899, setting out from Liverpool. This occurred in that year's Parliamentary recess time.[58] At the same moment, great, far-reaching events were taking place in southern Africa as the British Government endeavoured to outflank the Boer farmers into firing the first shots in what became known as the Boer War, which commenced on 11 October 1899. So after a grand tour of the Canadian provinces, taking in such large towns and cities as Vancouver, Montreal, Ottawa, Winnipeg and Banff, an unexpectedly swift return to Britain was required, as Lloyd George wished to address the increasing South African crisis. In the process of departing from Canada or even in the excitement of such, Lloyd George managed to 'mislay' some of his personal items; 'three pairs of breeches in Montreal, a great coat left on a train, and similarly an amber cigar holder (which disappeared somewhere else), and his special P&O trunk from a wandering about in North America'.[59] His absentmindedness, or even carelessness, was not comparable with his fairly recent interest in foreign affairs. He had upheld the British Government's stance during the 1898 Fashoda incident with France in the Upper Nile Valley and earlier, he castigated Salisbury's Conservative Government for the 1896 Central American Land

Settlement (on terms not favourable to Britain) with the United States. Once the hostilities actually broke out in South Africa, Lloyd George's view was not totally imperialistic, nor was he either pacifist or warmonger. Essentially, his policy was to draw attention to the inequalities of the Boers' franchise arrangements and to the inept and clumsy course that the hostilities took, and that the war was unnecessary and expensive. On a national basis, he found he was fighting against a tide of imperial sentiment, which even filtered down to his own Parliamentary constituency. Even before he was back in England, he sent a message to his constituents in mid-September 1899, 'the prospect [of war] oppressed me with a deep sense of horror ... I shall protest with all the vehemence at my command against this outrage which is perpetuated in the name of human freedom'.[60] Lloyd George had decided he would oppose (and he turned out to be the principal objector) the war, and in so doing would take on the Conservative Party in general and, as will be seen, the Colonial Secretary, Joseph Chamberlain, in particular. He also managed to worry sections of the Liberal Party, especially Lord Rosebery. In Parliament, his stance was not popular in the prevailing patriotic climate, nor did he do measurably better in the later speech in Carmarthen where he wanted to protest against the infamy of war 'and here I do it [speaking against the war] tonight, even if I leave Carmarthen tomorrow without a friend'.[61]

Lloyd George's next actions effectively underscored his efforts as an investigative politician. He decided to deride men of good wealth who invariably lent their names to (dubious) business opportunities, and so began his attack on the Colonial Secretary, Joseph Chamberlain. Lloyd George's doubts about Chamberlain's financial probity went back to 1895, and after some investigation, Lloyd George took the moment of the 'Throne Speech' debate in Parliament for an assault on 'England's Tawdriest Statesman'. The Chamberlain family (of whom Lloyd George had harboured suspicions for some time), Lloyd George maintained (after some research), were large shareholders in Kynochs of Birmingham, the Small Arms Factory, Hadrian and Son, Tubes Ltd, Elliot's Metal and the Birmingham Trust Company – all of which were the Government's arms suppliers. Lloyd George tried to persuade the House to accept that all officers of the Crown should 'divest themselves of shares in firms [and resign directorships] that might create benefits from public contract'. Lloyd George also raised the suggestion that Sir William Houldsworth's vote cast for the North West Railway Company Bill be disallowed, as Houldsworth was both a director and shareholder in the company. He also attacked Members of Parliament for gaining personally from the Agricultural Land Rating Bill, Henry Chaplin being named in particular.[62]

In Parliament the merits or otherwise of a conflict were seriously debated, with Lloyd George scoring points against Colonial Secretary Chamberlain and the army generals. Lloyd George's probing questioning and attack were pointedly, at first, financial, 'the whole country ... has been told of the 'intolerable' situation in the Transvaal – well the wages of miners over there were four times higher than miners earned here ... there the [Transvaal] state exploited the mine capitalists by a Royalty tax of 50 per cent, here [in Britain] it was half of one per cent' (he remembered this when playing his famous War on Want and Poverty Budget of 1909). Wages of the mine kaffirs were addressed; 'it is preposterous to pay the present rate of wages to kaffirs [£2, 5 shillings] and as far as mining investors were concerned, one American businessman had estimated that Consolidated Goldfield shares would gain over two million pounds with an annual dividend of 45 per cent'.[63] Lloyd George, with social aspects in mind, always vividly contended that every Lyddite shell exploding on the African hills was 'carrying away an Old Age Pension and the only satisfaction was that it killed two hundred Boers, fathers of families, sons of mothers – are you satisfied to give up your Old Age Pension for that?'[64]

The war went on with military failures for the British against a numerically inferior but better organised, mobile Boer army, including the infamous December 1899 Black Week and into the early part of January 1900. Thereafter, the British effected a better success rate and managed to relieve the besieged towns of Kimberley, Ladysmith and Mafeking, together with surrender of part of the Boer Command at Paardeberg. Lloyd George, whilst correctly pointing out to his ever-growing mob of howling critics, that he had never blackened the name of any British soldier, always insisted that his objections to the war were on the grounds that matters 'could be [peacefully] justified as a matter of policy' – the strength of the argument being reflected in the Liberal leader Campbell-Bannerman's famous views contained in the Methods of Barbarism speech. Meanwhile, Lloyd George, despite local concerns, as part of his election efforts planned a visit to speak at Penrhyn Hall, Bangor, a particularly hostile part of his own constituency. He wished to speak against the war and stated 'if the [local Liberal] Association still deprecate meetings, I shall resign my candidature as I cannot hope to succeed if I am shut up'.[65] He also uttered the following famous words, 'Five years ago [1895] the electors of Caernarvon Boroughs gave me a strip of blue paper, the certificate of my election, to hand to the Speaker of Parliament as your accredited representative. If I never again represent Caernarvon Boroughs in the House of Commons I shall at least have the satisfaction of handing back to you that blue paper with no stain of human blood upon it'.[66]

He felt that strongly about it and, as it transpired, the proposed Bangor meeting resulted in a near riot. The police were in full force, and whilst there were interruptions, the local stewards kept reasonable order. Even so, some damage was caused and upon exit from the hall, Lloyd George was nearly lynched. However, Lloyd George's skilful oratory led to this resolution condemning the war being carried by a large majority. This was achieved, to a large extent, by extolling Chamberlain's (and his family members') financial benefits arising from the war itself. Lloyd George believed the Boer War could be renamed 'Chamberlain's War' and it was 'damnable' because it was unnecessary. Brave men's lives were being 'senselessly, needlessly, callously, sacrificed on the alter of one man's selfish ambition'.[67]

Lloyd George made his most telling point as the War Office, explained Lloyd George, had invited tenders for army cordite ammunition and seven tenders were received, ranging from 1 shilling 10 pence in the pound, to 2 shillings and 6 pence in the pound, the latter being from the Birmingham firm of Kynoch's. This was accepted, although after some negotiation, adjusted to 2 shillings and 3 pence; why was this? Lloyd George proceeded to confirm that there were family connections with Kynoch's; was this the same man [i.e. Joseph Chamberlain] who had the audacity to go to war with the Transvaal because (he said) President Kruger had enriched himself, similarly, by a dynamite monopoly.[68] Chamberlain responded by saying he had sold his own Kynoch shares prior to taking public office; but not so, as Lloyd George ascertained, for shares were still held in his family's names.

The same issue, Lloyd George continued, applied to the Admiralty contractors, Haskins & Sons; the majority shareholders were Mary Endicott Chamberlain (Joseph Chamberlain's wife), Arthur Neville Chamberlain, Joseph Austin Chamberlain (Member of Parliament and a paid official at the Admiralty) and certain lesser Chamberlain family members. Yet, Joseph Chamberlain was on record as saying that he had no interest, direct or indirect, in any firm dealing with the Government. It would appear Lloyd George's arrow had found its mark. In the meantime, the British were at last gaining the upper hand over the Boers (British shortcomings were already voiced by many, including the leading socialite Emily Hobhouse, the Liberal leader, Campbell-Bannerman and of course Lloyd George himself), and the Conservative Government decided to exploit their temporary popularity. Thus, on 17 September 1900, Parliament, courtesy of an aged and ailing Queen Victoria, was dissolved. The way was now clear for the so-called 'Khaki Election'.

Lloyd George had to strongly battle in his own constituency, facing inevitable taunts of being 'pro-Boer'. An effigy of Lloyd George was burned in each of the three major towns in his constituency including his traditional base at Cricieth. However, at Bangor, where a few months before he would have been chased out of town, he turned an initial hostile crowd, as indeed he did at nearby Nefyn, by his infectious rhetoric attacking the Unionist Government's social reform records and suggesting all wars were 'horrible in their incidence' and 'to bring it [the War] to an end the better it is'. Overall, his tactics paid off, as on election day, Saturday 6 November 1900, Lloyd George was returned once again as the MP, with an increased majority of 296 – exactly 100 more than in the 1895 contest. Arguably, his twin approach of drawing attention, repeatedly, to Chamberlain's family benefiting from arms sales and Lloyd George's own persuasive oratorical powers defending his principled stance on the war, paid electoral dividends.[69] Naturally enough, Chamberlain resisted Lloyd George's 'war profits' insinuations and defended himself accordingly, in the House of Commons. He explained, as far as his own commercial dealings were concerned, 'I find it hard ... to stand here and explain to my colleagues on both sides of the House that I am not a thief and a scoundrel'.[70] The ceasing of the Boer War hostilities, ended effectively by the Treaty of Vereeniging of 1902, nevertheless, did mark some serious turning points in Lloyd George's political career. He was now, very much, the man to be watched on the Liberal benches – famous for his principled stand, especially with the party leader Campbell-Bannerman over the Orange River Camps, and much famed for his exposures of the Chamberlain family's war profiteering. The said Camps, dubbed Concentration Camps, were used to imprison Boer soldiers, and later their families, where overcrowding, disease, death, and simply bad administration meant sizeable, needless Boer deaths. Emily Hobhouse visited from Britain to assess the situation and immediately found herself at odds with General Kitchener, as indeed did most of the Liberal Party, including Lloyd George and Campbell-Bannerman, over the entire 'Methods of Barbarism' employed.

During this time, Lloyd George also began his lifelong friendship with Winston Churchill, and Lloyd George's equally strong detestation of the Harmsworth Press empire dates from this time. Whilst the hostilities in South Africa spluttered on to a final conclusion, Lloyd George saw an advantage beginning to appear. After discovering that the *Daily News*, the most popular Liberal newspaper in the country, was in financial difficulties, Lloyd George persuaded some affluent leading Liberals, including the prosperous chocolate making Cadbury brothers, to raise enough capital to buy out the hard-pressed *News*, then clearly intended to become a useful tool in pressing home his political views. Additionally, George Cadbury had been induced by Lloyd George to acquire a major shareholding in the process. Lloyd George found himself a director under the new proprietors in conjunction with Rudolf Charles Lehman and most of the existing newspaper's (Unionist leaning) staff were replaced by new Liberal-minded alternatives. The cost of this operation was £100,000, further working capital was needed of £30,000, and this was all in place by early 1901. At last, a sizeable (with the new ownership and increased readership), Liberal-owned newspaper was available to assist in reviving the previously divided Liberal Party, with Rudolf Lehman appointed as editor.[71] On a personal basis, Lloyd George was paid a 'negotiation fee' of 1,000 guineas, so reported his son Gwilym, 'to enable the family to live comfortably for five years'.[72]

Most importantly, Lloyd George now had 'a platform to proclaim his views'. Campbell-Bannerman, who was less enthusiastic, at least initially, fearing another divisional aspect within party ranks, was nevertheless reassured by the editorial keynote being 'party unity, no recriminations, no attacks on friends, but valiant attacks on the Unionist Government'.[73]

Lloyd George made the most of the Government's explanation of Boer war costs, again utilising his oratorical invective on the theme of misspent taxes. 'Fifty thousand horse and foot sent to Table Bay [in South Africa] and ten million of money will settle the whole thing ... grievously in error ... we have had to treble the number of men and we want another thirteen millions of money ... really it has cost us more than we ever thought ... Parliament was asked for another forty-six million ... [by] September 1900 ... after the war had been officially over there was an election ... Unionists went back into office ... discovered another mistake ... more money was voted in December, January 1901 and February 1901 ... voting so many millions lately. Now there is a fund for the old, broken, and poor – how many houses could you build to shelter them from the winter storms? How many could you save from the pauper's tomb of the real soldiers of the field – fifty-six millions of money – to be blazed away in fireworks in South Africa?'[74]

Effectively, his party-unifying speeches were rather more than the earlier disruptive concepts, and were beginning to succeed, although he nearly lost his life in the much publicised appearance in the summer of 1901 to address the party faithful at Birmingham Town Hall. Despite his endeavours and a strong police truncheon charge, he had to flee the hall dressed as a policeman as forged ticket holders and other ruffians broke through the official police cordon to wreck the hall, throw bricks (and other missiles), fight and hurl stones wrapped in barbed wire. His speech hardly started and much to Maggie's relief, he later returned to her, alive and well, but somewhat chastened by the experience. A month after this 'riot' Lloyd George discovered that the Chief Constable of the City was an Irishman and had imported a fierce band of tall Irish recruits into the police force for this very meeting – some of whom were, apparently, strong pro-Boers and hence the ferocity of the police baton charge.[75]

By 1902, Lloyd George had switched his political attention to schoolchildren, and in particular contested the Balfour Education Bill's provisions in the unappealing national (Church of England) schools, attended by Welsh non-conformist pupils. What really irked

Baptist and Methodist parents was the provision of local authorities (invariably Liberal), who would be compelled to financially keep such schools in good repair, i.e. a burden on the rates paid by all ratepayers and thus by all shades of religious belief. Nevertheless, in the committee stage of the Bill, Lloyd George's wily mind now obtained approval to the effect that a local authority need not take over the (ongoing) maintenance of a school if the school building in question had not been kept in proper state of repair. How exactly would local councils interpret that? In any event, he needed to retain the support of English non-conformists, 'control is what we want – the cure of that is the appointment of teachers – the schools would then be free'. In June 1904, Lloyd George received word that active English support had been forthcoming; the West Riding of York County Council voted unanimously, 'a resolution in favour of the adoption of Welsh policy'.[76] This stance followed the Liberal Party sweeping to a great victory in Wales by way of the County Council elections that year. Lloyd George's own *Daily News* added, 'Wales stands together – she threw down the glove to the [Welsh Convention of County Council Representatives] Board of Education at Cardiff – let the Board take it up if they dare'.[77]

Megan, the last Lloyd George infant, was safely delivered at Cricieth on 22 April 1902. Also, as some sign of financial improvement, a housekeeper and maid were now employed at the Lloyd George London home(s) of Trinity Road and then 3 Routh Road. Not long afterwards, the Lloyd Georges suffered a personal tragedy; Richard Owen, Maggie's father, died on 2 November 1903 and left his wife Mary an estate valued at £1,558 2s 6d. His will indicated the estate would, on Mary's subsequent death (which occurred on 27 May 1907) in turn pass on to Maggie, who would then have some asset value in two homes.[78] Amidst this sadness, the prospect of Lloyd George's Parliamentary fortunes began to take an upward turn. Politically, the Unionists were struggling to maintain their structure, and Liberal cohesiveness now looked remarkably apparent.

Most of Lloyd George's prominent biographers point out that the period 1903-1905 takes Lloyd George to the ultimate point of his political strengths, effectively positioning himself between the old Gladstonian ideals, with a flavouring of non-conformist zeal, education and Temperance (old Liberal) policies and embracing the new Liberalism with more than an accent of social reform. This was always underpinned by his superb tactical orations. His own finances, required essentially for family maintenance and expenditure, were now slipping into slightly better waters. Despite the setback of legal business (and hence the disappearance of professional fees) following his much publicised anti-Boer War image (carefully avoiding any blame towards the average British soldier) legal work began to pick up again, with both Lloyd George and George in Wales and Lloyd George & Co. in London now moving into partially greater profitability. The 'woefully scanty' legal profits throughout 1897 and 1898 were much in the recent past.[79] Undeniably, due to Lloyd George's ongoing verbal assaults on the Balfour Government, now tottering (as it turned out) into its last days, Lloyd George suffered a severe throat infection, which, in due course, led to his tonsils being removed.[80] Now a complete break was recommended and the two Lloyd George brothers set off to Genoa in Italy for six to eight weeks, holidaying. In the event of news of the Balfour Government's imminent collapse, the plan was that Lloyd George would return first and summon his brother David when the long awaited developments of the dying days of the Tory Government would be beyond speculation. As 1904 edged towards 1905, Lloyd George could feel much enheartened with great satisfaction following the arrival of a new lifelong colleague, admirer and fellow maverick politician, Winston Spencer Churchill. He was disillusioned with the Unionist Party's Tariff Reform ideas and crossed over to the Liberal front benches full of Free Trade members. In Caernarfon, Churchill, speaking from the same platform as Lloyd George, declared his new colleague, 'the best fighting General of the Liberal Army'.[81] In the closing days of 1904 Lloyd George reports, in a letter to his brother, that a close friend, Herbert Lewis and fellow Liberal MP (Flint Boroughs 1892-1906), 'Wants me to sail with him to Naples on 16 December [for a three week holiday] – he will pay my passage – I hate the sea but it will do me good'. As Brynawelon in Cricieth was let (and rent received) Maggie and the children spent that Christmas at Garthcelyn, William George's nearby home.

As it was, politically, the years 1904 and 1905 also heralded the final stages of Liberal revolt against the Unionists' 1902 Education Act that, fortuitously or otherwise, coincided with the Welsh religious revival and nationally also reflected the dying stages of the Unionist

Government eventually going out of office, and this lasted until after the First World War. In his book on Lloyd George, Emyr Price argues that Lloyd George was wholly and truthfully involved in his support and encouragement of Welsh issues, only later turning to British national aspects, whereas other prominent historians – Grigg, Morgan and Graham Jones – perceive that Lloyd George's primary ambition was to conquer British national issues all along and merely used his absorption in Welsh matters as preliminary steps to a greater British goal with the Young Wales Movement's [*Cymru Fydd*] collapse in 1896 as an effective turning point, although it is equally fair to suggest that he never fully ceased to aspire to Welsh Home Rule.[82]

Clearly, Lloyd George was by now making a mark within the political arena, and with his various money-making schemes generating significant income, Boer War unpopularity could well have electorally unseated him but his strength of character, resolve, and moral stance over the war itself turned into vote-winning characteristics.

Notes

1. Donald McCormick, *The Mask of Merlin*, (MacDonald, London 1963), p.48.
2. Peter Rowland, *Lloyd George*, op. cit., p.60.
3. B.B. Gilbert, *David Lloyd George - A Political Life*, op. cit., p.60.
4. A full detailed examination of the Llanfrothen Burial Case can be found in Herbert Du Parcq, *Life of David Lloyd George*, Vol.2, op. cit., and J. Hugh Edwards, *The Life of David Lloyd George*, (Waverley, London, 1913), Vol.2.
5. Ffion Hague, *The Pain and the Privilege*, op. cit., p.104.
6. Richard Lloyd George, *My Father - Lloyd George*, op. cit., pp.42-43.
7. Ibid.
8. Olwen Carey-Evans, *Lloyd George was my Father*, (Gomer Press, Llandysul, 1985), p.64
9. B.B. Gilbert, *Lloyd George - A Political Life*, op. cit., p.75. Also see Richard Lloyd George, *My Father - Lloyd George*, op. cit., pp.42-43.
10. W.R.P. George, *The Making of Lloyd George*, op. cit., p.169.
11. J. Graham Jones, *David Lloyd George and Welsh Liberalism*, op. cit., p.28.
12. F.W.S. Craig, *British Parliamentary Election Results*, (Macmillan, London, 1974), p.453.
13. John Grigg, *The Young Lloyd George*, op. cit., p.84.

14. Don M. Cregier, *Bounder from Wales* - Lloyd George's Career Before the First World War, op. cit., p.35. See also Frank Owen, *Tempestuous Journey*, op. cit., p.52.
15. Roy Hattersley, *David Lloyd George - The Great Outsider*, op. cit., p.51.
16. Ffion Hague, *The Pain and the Privilege*, op. cit., p.117.
17. Frank Owen, *Tempestuous Journey*, op. cit., p.61.
18. K.O. Morgan (Ed.), *Lloyd George - Family Letters 1885-1936*, op. cit., p.29.
19. Ibid., p.28. In later years, Rendel let the Lloyd George family use his house in Brighton.
20. W.R.P. George, *The Making of Lloyd George*, op. cit., p.174.
21. Ibid., pp.174-175.
22. W.R.P. George, *Lloyd George - Backbencher*, (Gomer Press, Llandysul, 1983), p.73.
23. J. Graham Jones, *David Lloyd George and Welsh Liberalism*, op. cit., p.42(f).
24. Ibid., pp.96-97 and p.114.
25. K.O. Morgan (Ed.), *Lloyd George - Family Letters 1885-1936*, op. cit., p.50.
26. Frank Owen, *Tempestuous Journey*, op. cit., p.64. Also, in J. Hugh Edwards *Life of Lloyd George*, Vol.3, op. cit., 'guinea pigs are men who once have MP added to their name and then sell themselves to the highest bidder'.
27. See diary entry for 10 June 1890, K.O. Morgan (Ed.), *Lloyd George - Family Letters 1885-1936*, op. cit., p.28.
28. John Grigg, *The Young Lloyd George*, op. cit., p.174, via Inland Revenue records.
29. Roy Hattersley, *David Lloyd George – The Great Outsider*, op. cit., pp.70-71 and p.642.
30. K.O. Morgan, *Lloyd George - Family Letters 1885-1936*, op. cit., p.58.
31. B.B. Gilbert, *David Lloyd George – A Political Life*, pp.106-107, and N.L.W. MS.20410C.
32. Roy Hattersley, *David Lloyd George – The Great Outsider*, op. cit., p.90.
33. Ibid., p.91.
34. Ibid., p.92.
35. Ibid., pp.92-93
36. Ibid., p.93.
37. K.O. Morgan (Ed.), *Lloyd George - Family Letters 1885-1936*, op. cit., p.61.
38. See John Grigg, *The Young Lloyd George*, op. cit., pp.184-194 for the full story of the Patagonian Gold fiasco.
39. Roy Hattersley, *David Lloyd George – The Great Outsider*, op. cit., p.96. The final notice of dissolution appeared in the *London Gazette* on 5 November 1907.
40. See letter to wife (No. 746) N.L.W. MS.20413C – dated 2 November 1896.
41. See John Grigg, *The Young Lloyd George*, op. cit., pp.178-197. Also W.R.P. George, *Lloyd George - Backbencher*, op. cit., pp.107-135; and K.O. Morgan, *Lloyd George*, (Purnell, London, 1974), p.38.
42. John Grigg, *The Young Lloyd George*, op. cit., p.196, and Northern Assurance Letter to Lloyd George, 31 December 1894 – National Library of Wales (see

copy of Assurer's Life Committee Minutes dated 10 January 1895 confirming Lloyd George accepted as a risk for insurance purposes, Appendix 2).

43. K.O. Morgan, *Lloyd George*, op. cit., p.35, interestingly notes, 'Since his wife [Maggie] was anxious that he [Lloyd George] should remain an MP which inevitably meant lengthy stays in London'. Previously, immediately post-marriage in 1888, Maggie had looked forward to a stable, reasonably salaried life as a country solicitor's wife, based in north Wales.

44. F.W.S. Craig, *British Parliamentary Election Results 1885 – 1918*, op. cit., p.453.

45. W.R.P. George, *Lloyd George - Backbencher*, op. cit., pp.182-183.

46. Boris Johnson, *The Churchill Factor*, (Hodder & Stoughton, London, 2014), p.73.

47. Roy Hattersley, *David Lloyd George – The Great Outsider*, op. cit., p.106.

48. Richard Lloyd George, *My Father - Lloyd George*, op. cit., p.60

49. William George, *My Brother and I*, op. cit., p.204.

50. K.O. Morgan, *Lloyd George - Family Letters 1885-1936*, op. cit., p.111. See diary entry for 28 May 1897.

51. W.R.P. George, *Lloyd George - Backbencher*, op. cit., p.183.

52. *History of Lewes Golf Club*, (Lewes Golf Club, 1995).

53. W.R.P. George, *Lloyd George - Backbencher*, op. cit., pp.248-251.

54. John Grigg, *The Young Lloyd George*, op. cit., p.175.

55. Ibid., pp.194-195.

56. W.R.P. George, *Lloyd George - Backbencher*, op. cit., p.301

57. W.R.P. George, *Lloyd George - Backbencher*, op. cit., pp.241-245.

58. John Grigg, *The Young Lloyd George*, op. cit., p.251.

59. Ibid., p.253.

60. Frank Owen, *Tempestuous Journey*, op. cit., p.94.

61. Ibid., p.75.

62. Don M. Cregier, *Bounder from Wales*, op. cit., p.69. Also Martin Pugh, *Lloyd George*, (Longman, London, 1988), p.17. Lloyd George came to like and respect Chaplin especially in his capacity as Chairman of the 1899 Select Committee set up to investigate Old Age Pensions.

63. Ibid., p.97.

64. Roy Hattersley, *David Lloyd George – The Great Outsider*, op. cit., p.123.

65. Frank Owen, *Tempestuous Journey*, op. cit., p.99.

66. Roy Hattersley, *David Lloyd George – The Great Outsider*, op. cit., p.133.

67. Frank Owen, *Tempestuous Journey*, op. cit., p.101.

68. Ibid., p.102.

69. F.W.S. Craig, *British Parliamentary Election Results 1885 – 1918*, op. cit., p.453.

70. Frank Owen, *Tempestuous Journey*, op. cit., p.109.

71. W.R.P. George, *Lloyd George - Backbencher*, op. cit., pp.326-329.

72. Ffion Hague, *Pain and the Privilege*, op. cit., p.207(f).

73. Peter Rowland, *Lloyd George*, op. cit., p.150. Also Gladstone Papers, B.M. Add. MS.45987 (footnote 165).

74. Ibid., pp.157-158.

75. Herbert Lewis, Diary, 2 January 1902, National Library of Wales.
76. W.R.P. George, *Lloyd George - Backbencher*, op. cit., pp.374-375.
77. Ibid., p.397.
78. Probate document dated 19 January 1904, prepared by Messrs. Lloyd George & George, solicitors, Cricieth (copy in author's possession).
79. J. Graham Jones, *David Lloyd George and Welsh Liberalism*, op. cit., p.84.
80. Frank Owen, *Tempestuous Journey*, op. cit., p.144. Both Maggie and Lloyd George himself would have given great thanks to Mrs. Tim Davis as, on another occasion - at a friend's house - Lloyd George's tonsils began to bleed profusely and 'Mrs. Tim' immediately summoned a young Welsh throat specialist - Dr. Lloyd - to administer relief and who later suggested that without another 10 minutes without help, Lloyd George would have died. .
81. Ibid., p.139.
82. Emyr Price, *David Lloyd George*, (University of Wales Press, Cardiff, 2006), pp.183-184.

3

1905-1916
The Marconi Share Scandal
and the Premiership

*'He [Lloyd George] cheerfully acknowledged that he was indeed the
man who had given the nation's old folk [retirement] pensions'.*
Peter Rowland[1]

The Italian sojourn, from mid-November 1905, started well enough
and proceeded to Florence and Rapallo. There the Lloyd George
brothers, whilst staying at the Hotel Verdi, met an elderly English
gentleman who advised that Balfour's resignation was imminent.
William, as agreed earlier, promptly left to return home, reaching
London on 1 December 1905. A new Liberal ministry was, he
believed, days, possibly only hours away – a telegram was despatched
to brother David, who, in turn, came back to reach London on the
evening of 3 December. As events transpired, Balfour resigned the
next day,[2] and Campbell-Bannerman, the Liberal leader, kissed hands
with the Monarch, Edward VII, and received the King's commission to
form a new Government. Much public and press speculation ensued,
including articles reviewing the ministerial prospects of David Lloyd
George. Previously, in March 1905, Lloyd George had written to his
uncle, Richard Lloyd, recalling his conversation with fellow MP John
Morley (Liberal, Montrose District of Burghs, 1986-1908) when
Morley foretold of Balfour's resignation somewhat earlier than when

it actually happened – stressing the information was confidential. Furthermore, Morley seemed to have good information, as Lloyd George's letter [to his uncle] concludes, 'I am to be in the Cabinet – that is settled'.[3] Strangely, there is no mention of these discussions in Morley's own memoirs of 1918, published by Macmillan of London, entitled *Recollections*. There were later talks with Morley on 6 July 1905 about a recent Lloyd George speech when Asquith was present. There was no mention of a subsequent future Cabinet position, although separate discussions with Morley again, dated 'sometime in late 1905' reveal Morley's comment to Lloyd George, 'If you take anything but Cabinet rank you will be a donkey'.[4]

Nevertheless, after the usual round of newspaper Cabinet placement mongering and rumours, the first idea was that Lloyd George was to get the Home Office (extremely unlikely as he did not have the right background or educational pedigree), with the Cabinet yearly salary of £5,000, or secondly, the Postmaster Generalship with a salary of £2,500 (Lloyd George declined this post) and latterly, which was the correct proposal, Lloyd George would be President of the Board of Trade at a salary of £2,000, with a seat in the Cabinet, albeit a junior one. Interestingly, the Liberal leader, Campbell-Bannerman was heard to grudgingly remark, 'I suppose we ought to include him'.[5] Lloyd George's brief covered areas such as labour troubles (memories of the Penrhyn slate workers' strike would be relevant), seamen, shipping, docks, harbours, foreshores, railways and bankruptcy. Clearly, his previous business ventures, as a young man in the ports of Barmouth and Porthmadog, could be of great use now. Essentially, Lloyd George's entry into the Cabinet was at the point when an uplift in income, now receivable as a Minister of the Crown, was fully needed.

With these new duties and the salary went the overseeing of ten department heads, 1,000 civil servants in all, plus the use of a ministerial car. So, after more than fifteen years as a radical in Parliament, Lloyd George, the youngest Cabinet Minister of 1905, commenced a run of Cabinet positions lasting seventeen more years. As Bentley B. Gilbert adequately summarises, 'he [a liberal rebel] who had always been a wrecker, had now become a builder'.[6] Put in another way, it was the first time since entering Parliament in 1890 that David Lloyd George was actually going to be paid for being a politician; a point not lost on the cash-strapped Maggie and family. Fortuitous timing as it transpires, being that the Lloyd George finances reflected he was now poorer than he had been in many years, as his legal practice income had suffered over his Boer War unpopularity. Indeed, Lloyd George had earned his spurs and, as the *South Wales News* – a Liberal newspaper, concluded; 'Moreover he had obtained Cabinet rank by sheer ability, force of character and, steady application'.[7] As to Lloyd George himself, whilst the appointment was at the lower end of Cabinet placements, he was convincingly pleased. He confided to his great friend, Charles Masterman (Liberal MP, West Ham North), 'when I [first] came to the Board of Trade I was in a blue funk – I thought here I am with no business training and I shall have to deal with all these great businessmen. I [later] found them children'.[8]

As an almost minor event in the Lloyd George household (which it was certainly not on a national basis) the ensuing January 1906 General Election followed, almost procedurally, which was called the 'Liberal Landslide'. Lloyd George simply romped home in Carnarvon Boroughs experiencing an ineffective challenge, with a hugely increased majority of 1,224 votes, trouncing the inexperienced Unionist opponent, R.A. Naylor. Maggie played a hugely prominent part in the constituency towards this success. In August 1906, a family holiday followed to Lisbon, and brother, William, was included. This family grouping enjoyed an upper-deck suite subsidised by Mr. Owen Phillips (Liberal MP for Pembroke and Haverfordwest, who, most usefully, was the director of several steam ship companies). Outside of politics, Maggie's fortunes expanded by way of property acquisition. Her mother died on 27 May 1907 and Maggie thus found herself the owner of two houses on the Porthmadog Road, Cricieth, namely Llys Owen and Brynawelon. Also, more financially relevant, Maggie was now entitled to the residue of her father's estate (he died on 2 November 1903) following the demise of her mother.

The London family home at Routh Road would seemingly never be quite the same again. Servants employed at the house were exclusively Welsh and invariably from Cricieth. All the maids were under the watchful eye of Sarah Jones (affectionately known in the family as Lally). Sarah remained with the family for fifty years. Lloyd George was always wary of her, as she could be quite outspoken.

Additionally, any kind of workers employed at Routh Road would have to be Welsh. One example of this is when James Evans, a master painter from Cricieth, was summoned to repaint the outside of the house, together with his assistant, young David, rather than using any London-based workman. Maggie always contended that Welsh workers produced a better job, and were happy with 'outer London' rates of pay! Moreover, James Evans mixed his own paints to give added permanency.

To his credit, Lloyd George brought a whole new meaning to his understanding of economics, at a national level, at least those socio-financial aspects of his Government work. Finding his way through the labyrinth of company law, patents, shipping, harbours, electricity and railways, undoubtedly aided by his legal background, business law experiences, simple pragmatism and negotiating skills, was no mean feat. He was ideally placed, indeed had learned from big businessmen such as Cadbury, Mond (also a golfing friend) and Crosfield, to hone these attributes into a three-way endeavour of merging business, labour relations and Government into a single unified task. He was moved to ask Walter Runciman (who was a junior minister and had shipping interest of his own), 'what can I do for commerce in the Board of Trade?'[9] Lloyd George made his own mark on the Board, by visiting harbours, manufacturing plants, North Sea ports and factories, to see for himself – not solely, as his predecessors had, relying on civil servants, papers, and views.[10] Vital economic areas of shipping (Plimsoll Line Bill), design (Patents and Dyes), and manufacturing (Books and Shoes) were the 1906 and 1907 highlights. These were followed by the Port of London Docks Bill of 1908, although in the latter instance, whilst Lloyd George was responsible for the creation of the Bill itself, it was Churchill, in his new position as President of the Board of Trade, that actually steered the legislation through the House of Commons. Each of these legislative items was praised at the time, although later analysis of the benefits to British shipping (Plimsoll Line) caused controversy and concern that the new laws were a pseudo attack on Liberal Free Trade principles. Equally, the Port of London amalgamation legislation, despite Asquith's experienced consultations and advice as a legal authority on Port matters, fell a little short of the desired objectives of merging the three main dock companies, namely the

Surrey Commercial, London & India, and Millwall Dock companies, which were locked in almost mortal combat for trade. Nevertheless, overall immediate plaudits from colonial governments, powerful businessmen, the national press – even the Kaiser, reportedly saying that Lloyd George was 'highly regarded in German business circles' – all added to Lloyd George's reputation[11] (although not so, never so in the eyes of his fellow Cabinet member, Reginald McKenna). There was a later allegation, unproved at least as far as the incomplete Port of London Authority (PLA) records show, to the effect that Lloyd George had acquired stock in the Surrey Commercial company, prior to the creation of the PLA itself at well below the £78 (per 100) price paid by the Government on amalgamation – the sum of £50,000 being suggested as Lloyd George's personal capital gain. He 'categorically denied that I have ever made any money out of London Docks'. Bentley Brinkerhoff Gilbert's book suggests that the profit might have been as much as £80,000.[12]

In the aftermath of the quite unexpected death on 30 November 1907 of Mair, the Lloyd Georges' eldest daughter, following a botched medical operation, both David and Maggie were grief-stricken and tortured with remorse beyond comprehension. In time, Maggie came to terms with Mair's death but Lloyd George himself never really did. This event only served to add to the existing gap of incompatibility between the two, which had been emerging for some time now. This extremely sorrowful event was undoubtedly a turning point in their marriage and relationship. Nevertheless, Lloyd George, despite heavy Board of Trade commitments, agreed to assuage his sorrow by taking a holiday in France. Lloyd George took Richard and Gwilym with him, but neither Olwen nor Megan – to an extent that a rift within the immediate family resulted. With Christmas looming, Maggie naturally preferred north Wales and the children. Whilst Lloyd George was away, Brynawelon was sold (and money realised) and Olwen and young Megan temporarily moved into Llys Owen, the parental home next door. Prior to his departure to the continent, Lloyd George made it clear he would not set foot in Routh Road again (where Mair had died) so Maggie rented a new London base at Cheyne Place in Chelsea, quite near to the old house of the Victorian sage, Thomas Carlyle. Margaret was also much involved in overseeing the building of a new family house, no doubt funded by the Brynawelon proceeds, in Cricieth, ready for occupation in late 1908. Privately, Maggie absolutely hated house moving. Both the old and new houses were called Brynawelon. Maggie was, nevertheless, keen to accept financial help, citing a similar offer made (and accepted) to Tom Ellis; Lloyd George countered by pointing out 'I have made up my mind not to – Tom Ellis did it and he was their doormat'.[13]

By late 1907, despite stunning political successes at the Board of Trade (especially Lloyd George's handling and ending of a railway dispute that year), the Lloyd George family seemed to be short of money. When his close colleagues discovered this, they proposed he be awarded an allowance from Liberal Party funds. To his credit, Lloyd George, on hearing this proposal, turned it down swiftly; 'I am not going to accept charity from the Party'.[14]

In that same year of 1907, Liberal ministers were becoming increasingly frustrated at the House of Lords, overwhelmingly Conservative, rejecting the Liberal Party's key legislative Bills; Education and Licensing were the main casualties. The Prime Minister, Sir Henry Campbell-Bannerman (1836-1908) channelled Liberal anger by putting down a motion in the Commons, during the 1907 Parliamentary session, to curtail the ongoing 'power of rejection' of key Bills severely, after passing through the Commons. Not much more was heard of this at the time and, by early 1908, Campbell-Bannerman had become terminally ill. He resigned the premiership in the first few days of April, to die a few weeks later, whilst still in 10 Downing Street. His obvious successor was Herbert Henry Asquith and, after first considering McKenna as a possible replacement as Chancellor, aware of Lloyd George's claim of superior experience, he initially asked the erudite pacifist, John Mosley, who preferred to happily remain in the India Office, thus leaving Lloyd George with no realistic challengers. Whilst having some misgivings, shared by the King, and indeed Asquith's wife Margot, nevertheless, no doubt believing his choice would meet favourable responses from the electorate, Asquith offered the position to Lloyd George. Roy Jenkins, in his study of Chancellors of the Exchequer from 1880 to 1945 commented about Lloyd George's tenure as Chancellor as 'an extraordinary phenomenon ... innovative [and] dazzling'.[15] Writing to his brother in celebratory mood, Lloyd George states triumphantly, 'I am [now] Chancellor of the Exchequer and, consequently, second in command of the Liberal host'.[16] Lloyd George well knew that his written words would be swiftly shown to his supremely supportive uncle in Cricieth. What is more is that this new post brought a much enhanced annual salary of £5,000 – and with it a lessening of the pressures of increasing living expenses to the Lloyd George household, the first of such immediate costings was the purchase of the official robes of office of the Chancellor, from Asquith.[17] Lloyd George's friend and confidante, Winston Churchill, was, as has been seen, promoted to the Board of Trade, the pair now being labelled in Parliament and the press as 'the Heavenly Twins'. Meanwhile, the Lloyd Georges moved into the official Chancellor's residence at 11 Downing Street – more expenses and even more semi-sour comment from Maggie (whilst proud of her husband's new challenge) over yet another house move.

The year 1908 was extremely significant for the Lloyd Georges' family economy. There was the new grace and favour residence of the Chancellor of the Exchequer, which for the Lloyd Georges dated from 6 April 1908, and personal expenditure was additionally pressurised to meet the £2,000 cost of building a second personally owned home (with the help of a mortgage), a virtual mansion also called Brynawelon in Cricieth. Indeed, there was also space enough to erect a small separate cottage, for a servant, gardener or chauffeur to use, in addition to the six guest bedrooms. Northcliffe, the powerful British press baron, tipped off Lloyd George that there were rumours circulating in London, later in 1908, that Lloyd George was financing the building of Brynawelon from profitable speculation in Port of London shares – as he put it, 'forewarned is forearmed'. Apparently, a little earlier Lloyd George had leaked some important information to Northcliffe, and this was his way of repaying that confidence. Separately, Lloyd George also told another press magnate, George Riddell, that the (originally £1,200) Brynawelon property represented 'his whole estate' and in any event was not yet fully paid for. The house was in Maggie's name.[18] Certainly, Maggie did not relish 11 Downing Street as a permanent abode, or at least whilst Lloyd George retained the Chancellorship, and continued to pay visits to her birthplace in Wales, using the building operations of the new Brynawelon as a first class reason to be there. Within the family, now that both Maggie's parents had passed away, an abiding friendship blossomed between her and Uncle Lloyd.[19] Nevertheless, the increased Cabinet salary for Lloyd George, made many things possible. Servants needed to be hired – Welsh speaking ones, of course. The children's ongoing education costings needed to be met and this meant fee-paying schools. The eldest, now deceased, Mair Eluned, was to study Mathematics at Cambridge. Olwen's schooling was transferred from Dr. Williams' school at Dolgellau to the Girls Public School at Roedean, near Brighton (now in East Sussex). This alternative choice was no doubt part influenced by Lloyd George's friendship with Lord (Stuart) Rendel of Hatchlands who owned a five storey house in Brighton at 2 and 3 Clarendon Terrace.[20] Olwen enjoyed her school days at Brighton (1908-1910) and school records reflect that the annual fees payable, ignoring the inevitable school extras, amounted to £81. Olwen's academic record at Roedean apparently was not remarkable although her best subject was German, and she was quite an effective lacrosse player.[21] She later attended Allenswood School, in south London, then Garret Hall in Banstead, Surrey, and then on to finishing school, abroad.

Megan, aged 6 in 1908, was similarly educated at Allenswood School and later at Garrett Hall School, Bansted, Surrey. Dick (Richard) had been to Dulwich College and later Porthmadog Grammar School and then moved on to Cambridge to study Engineering. Finally, Gwilym was finishing at Eastbourne College (annual fees at least £93), where he favoured sports and was in the school's Officer Training Cadet Force, which cost a further 15 shillings a term. He then moved on to Jesus College, Cambridge. Thus, private school fees, as evidenced in the case of Gwilym and Olwen, were now making inroads into the Lloyd George finances. In Megan's separate biography by Mervyn Jones, the start of Chapter 2 reports 'from this day [April 1908] onward the Lloyd George family always lived in easy circumstances'.[22] This is of course a very disputable statement.

Professionally, and financially, Lloyd George severed his legal connection with Lloyd George and George in 1908, although he had in reality ceased to practise from 1905. Politically, it was from 1908 (at least from August of that year, after Lloyd George had completed his fact-finding on social services aspects in Germany) that Lloyd George assuredly came to final prominence, by way of the 1909

Budget arrangements. The Budget speech itself was not especially well delivered in Parliament. Nevertheless, the Budget had the result of annoying both the brewing industry and the aristocracy, in each case bastions of the Tory Party – in matters of finance. Leaving precise details aside, in this study, the measures themselves could be summarised as increases in personal taxation and new liabilities introduced. The Lloyd George solution was based on his much publicised remark in 1908, 'I have got to rob somebody's hen roost next year ... where I shall get most eggs',[23] and the Peers believed that they had been singled out over the new Land Taxes. The essence of the dilemma to create more public finance was the need to fund the provision of Old Age Pensions, payable from January 1908, and simultaneously to meet the cost of the new large world-beating battleships, the Dreadnoughts to counter German naval expansion. Into the bargain, Lloyd George managed to irritate, into some exasperation, the King who was becoming more than a little frightened by Lloyd George's radicalism. His Majesty believed the Chancellor was impulsive, a view that was only slightly countered by the King's mistress Alice Keppel convincing King Edward that Lloyd George was, in reality 'an imperialist at heart'.[24]

It was Lloyd George's chance to use taxation to implement social change; something he had dreamed of as a young man having witnessed repression inflicted on the poor by the landed classes. For him, the 1909 Budget was a step in the right direction of equalising the classes in Britain and as he commented at the time, 'This is a war budget ... for raising money to wage implacable warfare against poverty and squalidness'.[25] The land-owning classes were not amused. Amongst the Budget debates, Lloyd George and his family plainly felt the blow of losing Mary Ellen, Lloyd George's sister, to cancer, on 9 August 1909. Maggie was very fond of Mary Ellen (Auntie Polly) who had always been very kind to the Lloyd George children. Lloyd George, conversely, over the years, became impatient with his sister's enthusiastic brand of religious puritanism. Mary Ellen was 47 years old and had been married to Philip Davies, a sea captain. Despite Lloyd George's own private grief and after paying a private visit to Cricieth for the funeral, he, nevertheless, sped off to Brighton the next weekend in the company of Charles and Lucy Masterman. Lloyd George's spirits had been lifted a little previously, when he was appointed Constable of Caernarfon Castle following Sir John Puleston's earlier death.[26]

Thus, by 1910, Lloyd George had enjoyed success as the Chancellor of the Exchequer and his own constituency majority at Carnarvon Boroughs now reflected healthy surpluses in the two 1910 General Elections (January 1910, 1,078 majority and December 1910 a little more at 1,208), underpinning his popularity. Indeed, most of Wales continued to vote Liberal, especially in the central areas and in the north; Flintshire, Pembroke, Anglesey, Arfon, Eifion, Carmarthen, Cardiganshire, and Radnorshire, invariably with no opposition for the second contest of 1910. Generally, Wales was a bastion of the Liberal cause. In May 1910, Edward VII died, and the ongoing Liberal Government, with the aid of Irish and Labour votes, now had the task of ensuring George V, as Edward's successor, would accept the inevitable new situation as proposed for the House of Lords' powers. Money matters, unlike the political arguments, disputes about trade, suffragettes, and personal storms ahead, looked well set fair, yet there were unexpected hurdles that needed surmounting, yet to surface. Again, allegations were made in *The People*, that Lloyd George could be named shortly as the co-respondent in a divorce case. What is more, the newspaper alleged that great efforts were made to 'hush up' the matter, estimating that the Chancellor of the Exchequer would have to part with £20,000. Lloyd George swiftly engaged the top law officers, Rufus Isaacs, F.E. Smith, and Raymond Asquith (the Prime Minister's son) to act on his behalf. Maggie was in court to hear Lloyd George insisting that the newspaper allegations were a total falsehood and the news editor apologised, offering damages of £1,000. The eminent MP, Edward Carson, was retained by the *People* newspaper. Lloyd George accepted the damages offer and used the said £1,000 nearly four years later as a gift to erect a new Village Hall near his birthplace in Llanystumdwy.[27]

Leaving such time-consuming actions aside, Lloyd George still sought out schemes to enhance his rather weak cash base. Another foray into a potential 'get rich quick' scheme reared its head, the possibility of financial exploitation of the Galician oil pipeline and oilfields. In this context, Lloyd George somewhat unwisely chose the spendthrift scoundrel Trebitsh Lincoln as his chief informant and adviser – a man with a record of financial disaster behind him.

Nothing came of this, as it transpired, and Donald McCormick summarises this association as an example of 'how the Welshman cultivated the strangest and most diverse personalities when he felt they could be of use to him'. By early 1911, Lincoln's creditors saw an opportunity to embarrass him by publishing his gross debt liabilities of £17,118.[28] Undoubtedly, Uncle Lloyd would have been appalled.

However improvident that may have been, Lloyd George's next financial arrangement had an element of clear sense in it. He took out a life assurance policy with Scottish Mutual (a life office specialising in teetotal policyholders) for £4,000 cover in the event of his death, from July 1910.[29] It could be taken that this measure was part of meeting the overall Brynawelon property and mortgage requirements as outlined earlier. Nevertheless, Lloyd George's living expenses were, additionally, added to by young Gwilym's private education costs. The boy was, as referred to earlier, a boarder at Eastbourne College in Sussex from 1910, and the termly fees worked out at £30 15 shillings. There were also added extra costs for music and, naturally enough, inclusion in the school's Cadet Officer Training unit. In annual terms, the total outlay would be virtually £100.[30] So, with Olwen's educational costs at Roedean, this meant the two children's private tuition costs were nearly £200 per year; more pressure on the Lloyd George purse.

In Parliament, the much-discussed National Insurance Bill progressed, strikes in major industries needed solving, suffragettes had to be reconciled, and above all, at least in Lloyd George's mind, there was a need for land legislation that he had always dreamed of. This meant revision of the machinery for fixed and fair agricultural rents, tenure of land, better terms for leaseholders and tribunals to determine fair wage levels on a district by district basis – in brief, the so-called Land Campaign. At the same time, the prospect of making money gains in the short-term once again reared its head. The origins of the aptly-called 'Marconi share scandal' began in the wake of the approval of the plan to erect a chain of state-owned wireless stations. These cost up to £60,000 each throughout the British Empire and were proposed in the aftermath of the discussions taken at the 1911 sixth Imperial Conference. Herbert Samuel, the Paymaster General, was instructed to investigate the entire position. After allegedly

61

looking at competitive systems, Marconi was selected. Even at this very early stage, no account seems to have been taken of the fact that the managing director of 'The Marconi Wireless Telegraph Company of London' was Mr. Godfrey Isaacs, the brother of Rufus Isaacs, the then Attorney General in the Liberal Government.

By the first quarter of 1912, the Marconi tender was reviewed and accepted by the Government (in spite of superior technical equipment available from America) although the specific terms of the arrangements, or contract, needed final approval by Parliament. On 9 April 1912 Godfrey Isaacs, on returning from America, where he had been involved in the sale of rights in the American company, lunched, in London, with his two brothers, Harry and Rufus. Godfrey Isaacs was directly responsible for the market placement of 500,000 American Marconi shares and in total confidence revealed this fact to his two brothers. Whilst Rufus Isaacs initially demurred, Harry Isaacs, sensing a financial opportunity, instantly acquired 50,000 of these new shares at £1 1s 3d per share. On hearing this, Rufus Isaacs then promptly changed his mind and took 10,000 of Harry Isaacs' new share allotment. A few days later, on 17 April, Rufus sold 1,000 of his shares to the ever eager David Lloyd George and a further 1,000 shares to the Scottish Peer, Alexander Murray, known as the Master of Elibank, then Chief Whip of the governing Liberal Party. No money changed hands at this point, nor did the shares get transferred, so technically, they did not exist, as it was only on 19 April, two days on, that these American Marconi shares were actually placed on the stock market, at a special launch price of £3 5s 0d per share, to rise to £4 exactly by the end of that day's stock market trading. Following further share transfer arrangements between two Isaac brothers and Lloyd George, the latter's share total increased to 1,286 ordinary shares. Lloyd George, sensing some profit, sold out on 20 April, as did Elibank, receiving £3 6s 6d per share, thus achieving a capital gain of £743 on the original but unpaid share price of £1 1s 3d. In brief, Lloyd George and his colleagues had acquired American shares at a discount, totally owing to privileged information and pre-launch availability. Additionally, they each must have assumed that Parliamentary approval of the Marconi contract itself, put before the House of Commons in July 1912, and by August, just before the annual recess, would then be simply a rubber stamped operation.

Herbert Samuel, the Postmaster General, commended the Marconi contract to the House of Commons on 7 August 1912. Meanwhile, Lloyd George, of course, was extremely occupied with the passage of the ongoing April 1912 Budget debates.

Nevertheless, as Lloyd George's correspondence to his wife at the time reveals, he could just not resist share speculation. He writes on 15 April 1912, 'So, you only have £50 to spare. Very well, I will invest that for you. Sorry you have got no more available as I think it is quite a good thing I have got', and a few days later on 19 April; 'Well, your spec. has come off and you have each of you made another £100. Llwydyn [Olwen] won't sell, as she thinks by holding out she will get more! I, also, made a few hundreds out of it so we are a little better off than we were at the beginning of the week'. On that same day, a second letter to Maggie reads, 'I got a cheque from my last Argentina Railway deal today. I have made £567 – but the thing I have been talking to you about is a new thing'.[31] This clearly demonstrates that Lloyd George (and family) had entered into share ownership and dealing, but something more than at beginner level. It is possible, though, that the reference in mid-April to share profit taking related to something other than Marconi stock.

Separately, Godfrey Isaacs had given assurances that the British and American Marconi companies were quite separate entities, regrettably failing to add that the former controlled the latter and that they shared the same patents and many other common interests.[32] In the second part of April and later on, on 14 May 1912, Lord Murray of Elibank significantly purchased a further 3,000 American Marconi shares costing £9,000, *using Liberal Party funds.* At this point, interestingly, Elibank promptly left politics to work in Bogotá, South America, quoting health as his reason for departure and hinted that there was, additionally, a reason for his departure 'only known to his colleagues' – most likely his dealings in Marconi shares.[33] This purchase remained hidden until the stockbrokers acting in the matter, Montmorency & Co., financially collapsed by default in June 1913 and the stockbroker's 'books' were then examined by the administrators. In that same month, on the 22nd, Lloyd George had purchased a further holding in American Marconi shares although, sadly for him, now in a falling stock market, yet he was no doubt encouraged by his claim of an earlier short term capital gain made on his initial allocation of stock. Thus, a further 1,500 (to make an adjusted total of 1,643) shares were bought in American Marconi at £230 more than the original costings in April 1912. Subsequently the stock value settled at around £200 per share. The equities in question were listed in his own name on the books of his stockbroker, Smith Rice & Co.

By July, rumours were in circulation that Marconi had been awarded the wireless station contract, merely because its managing director was the Attorney General's brother! More significantly, especially for Lloyd George, was the added innuendo that Government Ministers had been dealing in Marconi shares based on privileged information. The press now became involved and to some extent newspaper articles, such as the *Outlook* and *The Eye Witness*, were additionally basing their interpretation of events on an anti-Semitic conspiracy (the Isaacs brothers were Jewish). A further and more damaging article was published by the more widely-read *National Review*, headed by Leopold Maxse, a prominent Tory with more than a passing zeal for exposing Liberal Government misdemeanours. At this stage, in all probability, Prime Minister Asquith was in possession of all the raw facts, and he certainly was aware of the main details by the end of the year and had full knowledge by March 1913. As Frances Donaldson summarises in her penetrating book, 'no one would be likely to believe that men with nothing to hide would be content, week after week, to ignore public charges of the vilest corruption ... and in a more general tone [the Chancellor] and the Master of Elibank [who also obtained shares on behalf of the Liberal Party] have done what every novice punter indulging in a half guilty flutter does. They had bought half way up a boom and sold excitedly at a profit. Then at the first drop they bought again in larger quantities, on this occasion half way down a slump [in the share price]'. Separately, Elibank was also involved in shares acquired in John Dicks Ltd., who published *Reynolds News* in the flotation of 1911, which came to light in 1925 – a similar example of 'concealed investments'.[34]

More pointedly, the June 1913 issue of the magazine *Round Table* was quite damning; 'the Chancellor of the Exchequer is, in a sense, the ex-officio head of the City of London [Lloyd George might well have shuddered at that description]; for he is the highest financial officer of the British Empire. City opinion is therefore affronted by the disclosure of this sublime functionary behaving for all the world like the poor, greedy, excited Mr. Juggins of ordinary life'.[35] Undoubtedly, Uncle Lloyd, whilst immensely proud of his nephew's achievements, would have been equally horrified, if not feeling betrayed by Lloyd George's effective dishonour in the office of Chancellor. Clearly, there were shades of Lloyd George's earlier stance as regards Chamberlain and the munitions firm Kynoch during the Boer War. Apparently, Lloyd George did not necessarily appreciate the comparison at all.

Since Parliament had reassembled in October 1912, the Unionists dominated the Marconi debates, following exacting City gossip, pressing for the publication of the full Marconi contract details. Liberal Government Ministers acted, anticipating trouble. The Select Committee was still taking soundings into the decision to sign the Marconi contract and in Parliament one opposition member, George Lansbury (Labour, Poplar) asserted that Government Ministers had feathered their own nests.[36] Lloyd George angrily rose to the bait and demanded an explanation. In turn, Rufus Isaacs hastily confirmed, in those now famous words that 'neither he, nor the postmaster general, nor the Chancellor of the Exchequer had had one single transaction with the shares of that [English Marconi] company'. Even so, there were some mutterings about a Jewish conspiracy amongst the political classes, with some added rumours that British taxpayers had somehow been defrauded.[37]

In April and May 1913, polite Parliamentary language was being stretched when Lloyd George was asked by J.R. Kebty-Fletcher (Unionist, Altringham, Cheshire), 'Is not the Right Honourable Gentleman's salary sufficient to prevent him from wrongfully, and improperly gambling [in Marconi shares]?' At this point Lloyd George leapt to his feet, eyes blazing, suggesting if that was repeated – 'it will be in a place where he would be subject to cross-examination'.[38]

This was, effectively, a form of words uttered to deceive. Both Ministers showed little interest in testifying before the Commons appointed multi-party Select Committee, and each felt unable to answer the charges levied against them for several months. At last, Lloyd George did, on 28 March 1913. This was when Lloyd George claimed he was a modest, humble, and poor man, living on his £5,000 ministerial salary with a [£2,000] property in Wales [in Maggie's name] and investments producing about £400 per year. He concluded, 'That is my great fortune' and immediately flourished his dispatch case to exhibit, if need be, the contents of his own and Maggie's passbooks. In addition, he offered, if required, sight of his brother's investment details.[39] In any event, he always claimed that any investments he made were for future income and not for speculation! The committee subsequently divided to report its overall findings and emerged with three quite different report versions, reflecting party lines. Asquith was well aware of Lloyd George's importance to the Government (seeing the National Health Insurance Bill through Parliament was a clear example, and dealing with suffragettes and women's voting aspirations another), even, in extremes, to its survival. Whilst not a convincing situation, Asquith's subsequent Parliamentary support in the ensuing debate on the committee's findings helped garner enough votes to partly exonerate the Ministers concerned, even condoning their actions to end the 'Marconi affair' – and retain Government Ministers' careers.

If Lloyd George believed he had been manoeuvred by his Marconi involvement into a tight corner, he had, as he told George Riddell (after 1920, Lord Riddell), news of other allegedly damning evidence in his 'locker to fling', if need be, at the Unionists. He is recorded as saying,

'I am going for them in the [Parliamentary] debate on the [Marconi Committee] report. I am going to show up [Lord] Selborne's transactions with the P&O of which he was a director while a member of the Government, [Arthur – later Earl] Balfour's dealings in Whittaker Wrights shares, [Sir Michael, later Viscount St. Aldwyn] Hicks-Beach's sale of his land at an outrageous price to the Government and Joe [Chamberlain's] transactions to the Niger Company of which he was a large shareholder'.

Even so, Lloyd George was reluctant to attack Joe Chamberlain separately because he was sizeably incapacitated following a severe stroke (and was later to die in 1914). Balfour, who was a notable 'investment adventurer' dismissed Lloyd George's threats when they came to his notice as 'childish' ideas. Nevertheless, Balfour lost some £1,000.[40]

In brief, whilst Ministers were obliged to admit their Marconi investments were really ill-chosen in the circumstances, it would have been more open to disclose the full range of facts to Parliament much sooner, although any charges against their honour and integrity were dissipated. Indeed, Balfour, the Unionist (opposition) leader, even dismissed allegations of the corruption as 'perfectly futile from the beginning and unworthy of the consideration of the House'.[41] Asquith was being more than a little disingenuous, yet maintained his Ministers' honour absolutely unstained; whilst strongly urging Lloyd George to be similarly contrite. In essence, Lloyd George had 'escaped the consequences of [his] behaviour, which was disreputable though not dishonest, as he had so often escaped the consequences of personal folly'.[42] Equally helpful was the level of restraint exercised by the Unionist leaders, well conscious of, if not embarrassed by, the serious anti-Semitism underlying any criticisms of Ministers.

During the ongoing Marconi affair, Lloyd George entered into his adulterous relationship (he referred to this as his second marriage) by way of his new secretary and subsequently mistress, Frances Stevenson, a former teacher, from early 1913. Frances, ironically, was introduced innocently enough to Lloyd George by his daughter, Olwen. The initial secretarial task he set her, without success, was to trawl through the newspapers of the day looking for any Marconi reference or reports, thus accessible to the general public, as regards the suitability and more importantly any availability of the American Marconi shares. Frances was an excellent choice for such an assignment with her built-in confidentiality, basic secretarial experience, linguistic expertise and other existing research skills. Frances records, in her 1967 autobiography, 'so great was the power and mastery that he [Lloyd George] already exercised over me that I did not doubt for one moment that he was in command of the situation – he made me realise that I was *necessary* [author's italics] to him'.[43] On a personal financial basis, the Lloyd Georges could now undoubtedly be described as comfortably off: as Chancellor, Lloyd George's salary was £5,000 per year, the modern equivalent of this being about £425,000. The Marconi Select Committee had been shown his portfolio, namely his Ministerial salary, and a modest income from investments – but what else? Only the small house in

Wales (Brynawelon) at a cost of just over £2,000, and 'the house where he lived at Walton Heath belonged to someone else'.[44] The newspaper baron Riddell had provided a house in late 1913 for Lloyd George at Walton Heath, Surrey, as a convenient near retreat from London. It was adjacent to the golf course, and Churchill, Illingworth (the Chief Whip) and Masterman all wanted houses there too! Angry suffragettes had already partly blown up this near-built property, and only poorly laid timing devices failed to create even more damage. Whilst not personally involved, a suffragette leader admitted that she had incited her followers to make this attack. She received a sentence of three years penal servitude for this crime.[45]

In this immediate post-Marconi period, Frances was to see Lloyd George as her protector and lover, who faced the political difficulties of labour unrest, the Irish home rule issue, and agitation for the female suffrage. Additionally, his main task as Chancellor of the Exchequer was to balance the nation's books with the ever increasing and competing claims for money from equally ever eager Government department Ministers. What better way to bring Liberals back together and to act as a diversion than to introduce his longed for and cherished ideology of a land campaign, including an elaborate study by experts. Equally, how could he use this ploy in the annual Budget announcements effectively to start this new drive for popular interest? Interestingly enough, by mid-1913, Lloyd George had managed to persuade Joseph Rowntree to part with £10,000 towards the land campaign's administration expenses.[46] Additionally, he had to worry about Churchill's (now at the Admiralty) aggressive campaign for increased finance for the Dreadnought construction programme (this issue was to cause some strain on the Lloyd George/Churchill friendship), which bedevilled Lloyd George's finite national tax calculations. Consequently, his 1914 forward Budget calculations were thrown sideways and Lloyd George's actual Budget statement in the House on 4 May 1913 was believed, by all those present, to be something akin to a disaster. A change in the legislative timetable seemed the only way ahead. Lloyd George, usually full of fight and vigour, blamed the Parliamentary draftsmen, even the Speaker of the House, for this outcome. Moreover, his own party colleagues' enthusiasm was waning, although his newspaper proprietor friend, Lord George Riddell, opined that Lloyd George's 'courage and powers of endurance are wonderful'.[47] These were excellent qualities indeed, but would they be enough?

Whilst the Marconi share affair was the most sensational Parliamentary happening of 1913, other more nationally important issues were commanding attention, namely the Cabinet in-fighting over increased naval expenditure and how to cost out Lloyd George's pet scheme of land re-rating and taxation. Separately there was the ongoing issue of Irish Home Rule, in particular the position of Ulster. Increasingly industrial difficulties were additionally emerging. Battleship (Dreadnought) expenditure would be covered, one way or another, in the 1913-1914 Budgets, by way of 'taxation adjustments' whilst Land Enquiry and subsequent legislation in the House would be spearheaded by Lloyd George. By October 1913, advance copies of the Land Enquiry report were distributed to those supportive Liberal newspapers, the *Liverpool Post, South Wales Daily News, Lancashire Daily Post*, the *Northern Echo, Manchester Guardian, Daily Chronicle* and, of course, Lloyd George's own favoured *Daily News*.

In the wake of Rowntree's land campaign donation, somewhat foolishly, Lloyd George waded in with criticism of *The Times* for its support of Royalty (rather than publicising the Land Reform proposals) but when King George V signified his offence, Lloyd George formally apologised by stating that he meant no disrespect to the Crown.[48]

So, leaving Ireland and the industrial agitation best illustrated by the 1912 coal strike, aptly covered in other works, the nation slowly slid to a war footing, with actual hostilities, despite Foreign Secretary Grey's endeavours, commencing on 4 August 1914. This was preceded by J.A. Spender's 'time of extraordinary bitterness in British public life'.[49] In Britain, a party truce was announced, and any hopes, however vague, of General Elections, postponed. The Cabinet, which had not been totally committed to war, was finally swayed by Germany's invasion of Belgium and the immediate imposition of the Defence of the Realm Acts legislation enabled Government control over economic matters and certain individual liberties, including press censorship. Lloyd George engineered these new wartime regulations in his capacity of Chancellor and supported Foreign Secretary Grey. Lloyd George had a low opinion of Kitchener, particularly underlined by his dealings with him over munitions production (in reality, lack of) in 1915.

The ongoing process of the (Great) War was beginning to be questioned. Despite his decision to obtain Lloyd George's agreement to leave the Chancellorship (inherited by McKenna) and move over to head the newly created Ministry of Munitions, Asquith, clearly, was not firm enough in his direction of the war, preferring to leave major policy issues to the generals. Even they, especially the French command and Kitchener, were at loggerheads. At one point, Lloyd George floated the idea of the Government purchasing the trade interests of the drink trade for the nation at £300 million, but this lacked Cabinet enthusiasm.[50]

Lloyd George's tenure at the newly formed Ministry of Munitions was short enough, although it took only a little time for Lloyd George to realise that, in particular, the artillery shell production, either high explosive or shrapnel, were on the wrong lines and not serving the interests of the front line soldiers in France. Kitchener believed Lloyd George was as culpable as was equally, the German-sounding Sir Stanley Von Donop (Head of Ordnance) as regards the manufacture and distribution of artillery, or rather the lack of it, on an efficient basis. The infantry battles in Flanders and the wrong footed and badly organised Gallipoli adventure all added into a feeling of a change of direction being required at the top. As 1915 passed into 1916, the army stalemate in France, most infamously on the Somme, ground its deathly way forward. Kut in Mesopotamia was surrendered to the Turks, Lord Kitchener was drowned just off the Orkneys and the naval battle of Jutland, with its non-decisive result (save for keeping German ships in port) and the submarine menace increased. At home, the Easter rebellion in Dublin caused a major distraction to the war effort in Flanders. 'Send Lloyd George to the War Office', was one particular cry. Rows about compulsory military service, namely conscription, were now increasingly arising.

In brief, the Liberals needed help – firstly a Coalition with Conservatives was orchestrated, but by 1916 this was not enough and the major change of Asquith resigning on 5 December 1916, to be succeeded by Lloyd George, happened, after much manoeuvring, by 7 December 1916. Lloyd George was now Premier – salary unchanged at £5,000[51] (this had been static since 1831!), with the additional 10 Downing Street property occupation benefit. By the Friday, 8 December, Margot Asquith wrote with some practicality, to Maggie Lloyd George, asking if she and her husband, H.A. Asquith, be allowed to remain in 10 Downing Street for two weeks, to give time for them to find a new house. The Lloyd Georges readily agreed, with Lloyd George himself stating that he would continue to live at 11 Downing Street for the foreseeable future. Nonetheless, shortly after this, Asquith drove down to his retreat at Walmer Castle in Kent, not to return. Certainly, where the Asquith family might live (in London) was the pressing problem after, as Colin Clifford puts it, 'their abrupt ejection from 10 Downing Street'.[52]

Margot Asquith never forgave Lloyd George for 'ousting' her husband from the Premiership and, for some years after 1916, equally never failed to score points against Lloyd George. Cabinet positions were now re-aligned once more to effect a virtual balanced Liberal/Conservative flavour.

Lloyd George had, consequently, arrived at the Premiership of Great Britain; something that had crossed his mind as a young boy. His uncle Richard (not long for this earth) was thrilled. Financially, Lloyd George's major sources of earnings would now be taken to a broader horizon.

Notes

1. Peter Rowland, *Lloyd George*, op. cit., p.203
2. J. Graham Jones, *David Lloyd George and Welsh Liberalism*, op. cit., p.86. Also Peter Rowland, *Lloyd George*, op. cit., p.182. Lloyd George, with a sneer, retorted, "they died with their drawn salaries in their hands".
3. J. Graham Jones, *David Lloyd George and Welsh Liberalism*, op. cit., p.86.
4. K.O. Morgan (Ed.), *Lloyd George - Family Letters 1885-1936*, op. cit., pp.142-143.
5. Martin Pugh, *Lloyd George*, op. cit., p.39. Another theory was that Lloyd George's inclusion was a sop to Welsh MPs.
6. B.B. Gilbert, *David Lloyd George - A Political Life*, op. cit., p.284.
7. *South Wales News*, 11 December 1905.
8. Frank Owen, *Tempestuous Journey*, op. cit., p.148.
9. Don M. Cregier, *Bounder from Wales* - Lloyd George's Career Before the First World War, op. cit., p.103.

10. Lloyd George, additionally, did not forget his past Welsh contacts. David R. Daniel (1859-1931), the former Secretary of the North Wales Quarrymen's Union, kept Lloyd George updated on union organisation in quarries up to 1906, and then took a post as a second secretary to the Coast Erosion Committee – he later became estranged from Lloyd George during the Great War of 1914-1918. See R. Mervyn Jones, *The North Wales Quarrymen 1874 – 1922,* (University of Wales Press, Cardiff, 1981), p.203.

11. Don M. Cregier, *Bounder from Wales* - Lloyd George's Career Before the First World War, op. cit., p.109.

12. John Grigg, *Lloyd George from Peace to War 1912-1916,* (Methuen, London, 1985), p.47 and footnote. Also B.B. Gilbert, *David Lloyd George - A Political Life,* op. cit., p.37

13. Ffion Hague, *The Pain and the Privilege,* op. cit., pp.186-187.

14. Roy Hattersley, *David Lloyd George – The Great Outsider,* op. cit., p.217.

15. Roy Jenkins, *The Chancellors,* (Macmillan, London 1998), p.165.

16. William George, *My Brother and I,* op. cit., p.220. Letter dated 11 April 1908. Lloyd George had performed well at the Board of Trade, and deserved promotion. He was lucky to become Chancellor this early in his career.

17. Don M. Cregier, *Bounder from Wales* - Lloyd George's Career Before the First World War, op. cit., p.113.

18. Ibid., pp.137-138. Also, Frank Owen, *Tempestuous Journey,* op. cit., p.196, and B.B. Gilbert, *David Lloyd George - A Political Life,* op. cit., p.399.

19. Viscount Gwynedd, *Dame Margaret,* (George Allen & Unwin, London, 1947), p.140.

20. Brighton Street and Business Directories, 1902-1913, Local Studies Library, Brighton.

21. Roedean School bursary records, inspected on 12 November 2010.

22. Mervyn Jones, *A Radical Life - Megan Lloyd George 1902-66,* (Hutchinson, London, 1991), p.15.

23. 1908 *Parliamentary Debates,* June 15, 23, and 29, House of Commons.

24. Don M. Cregier, *Bounder from Wales* - Lloyd George's Career Before the First World War, op. cit., pp.116-117.

25. 1909 *Parliamentary Debates,* April 29, House of Commons.

26. B.B. Gilbert, *David Lloyd George - A Political Life,* op. cit., pp.39-400.

27. See accounts of this in Peter Rowland, *Lloyd George,* op. cit., p.215. Also Roy Hattersley, *David Lloyd George – The Great Outsider,* op. cit., pp.234-235, and J. Graham Jones, *David Lloyd George and Welsh Liberalism,* op. cit., p.149.

28. Donald McCormick, *The Mask of Merlin,* op. cit., p.76.

29. Dominic Hobson, *The National Wealth,* (Harper Collins, London, 1999), p.997.

30. Eastbourne College Archives, 1910.

31. K.O. Morgan (Ed.), *Lloyd George - Family Letters 1885-1936,* op. cit., p.162. See also John Grigg, *Lloyd George,* op. cit., p.48.

32. Don M. Cregier, *Bounder from Wales* - Lloyd George's Career Before the First World War, op. cit., p.201.

33. John Grigg, *Lloyd George*, op. cit., p.50. See also John M. McEwan (Ed.), *The Riddell Diaries*, (Athlone Press, New Jersey, 1986), p.67.
34. Lady Frances Donaldson, *The Marconi Scandal*, (Quality Books, London, 1962), p.58.
35. Cited in John Grigg, *Lloyd George*, op. cit., p.62.
36. Peter Rowland, *Lloyd George*, op. cit., p.263. Also, Colin Clifford *The Asquiths*, (John Murray, London, 2003), p.209.
37. Ibid. p.264 (and many other publications). One also suspects Unionist politicians would have similarly acted.
38. Frank Owen, *Tempestuous Journey*, op. cit., p.233.
39. Ibid., p.232. This is a far cry from Lloyd George's apparent wealth, described by J.A. Spender in late 1920 as a 'bottomless purse': letter from Oswald Partington, Second Baron Doverdale to Spender of 9 November 1920.
40. John M. McEwan (Ed.), *The Riddell Diaries*, op. cit., p.65, entry for 31 May 1913. Also R.J.Q. Adams, *Balfour – The Last Grandee*, (John Murray, London, 2007), p.275.
41. John Simon, *Retrospect*, (Hutchinson, London, 1952), p.91.
42. Roy Hattersley, *David Lloyd George – The Great Outsider*, op. cit., p.329.
43. Frances Lloyd George, *The Years that are Past*, (Hutchinson, London, 1967), p.55.
44. Frances Donaldson, *The Marconi Scandal*, op. cit., p.126. Also Frank Owen, *Tempestuous Journey*, op. cit., p.233.
45. John M. McEwan (Ed.), *The Riddell Diaries*, op. cit., p.49 and p.59.
46. Stephen Koss, *The Rise and Fall of the Political Press in Britain* (Vol.2), (University of South Carolina Press, 1984), p.227.
47. George Riddell, *More Pages from my Diary*, (Country Life, 1934), p.27.
48. Stephen Ross, *The Rise and Fall of the Political Press in Britain*, op. cit., p.228.
49. Ibid., p.238.
50. John M. McEwan (Ed.), *The Riddell Diaries*, op. cit., p.107, 17 April 1915.
51. House of Commons Information Office, London. Reference 2013/2014/65/PCC. It is also understood that the basic MP salary from 1911, at £400 per annum, would not be payable in addition – see House of Commons Resolution of 10 August 1911.
52. George Riddell, upon seeing Margaret Asquith's letter, described the wording as 'oily and insecure'. See B.B. Gilbert, *David Lloyd George - A Political Life*, op. cit., p.419. Also Colin Clifford, *The Asquiths*, op. cit., p.386.

4

1916-1922
New Sources of Income

*'His methods are dubious, and his manners intolerable, but he has
a genius and an insight and absolutely amazing courage which places
him, in my opinion, high among the great rulers of our race; not even
excluding the elder Pitt, who also had grave defects of character'.*
Lord Alfred Milner (1854 – 1925)[1]

In early 1917, two events dominated Lloyd George's life. Firstly, the
Russian Revolution occurred, leading to the overthrow of the Tsar,
which added more pressure on the Prime Minister's war strategy.
Secondly, and extremely personally, Lloyd George lost his effective
foster father, advisor, and mentor, Uncle Richard Lloyd, who
passed away on 28 February 1917, dying of bowel cancer. He was
83 years old when he died. David Lloyd George's grief was genuine
and lasting. The pain of his passing was virtually intolerable and
Lloyd George desperately needed to fill the old man's place – perhaps
now only Frances Stevenson could undertake that role. Even so,
Frances was fighting her own personal battle of intense jealousy of
Maggie. Nevertheless, with Uncle Lloyd's passing, the remaining
link with Lloyd George's childhood and Cricieth was seemingly
removed. In effect, Lloyd George was entering, if not extending, the
period of his life reflecting a gradual breakdown of his relationship
with Maggie, as increasingly Frances was establishing herself
firmly in his life. Brother William George regarded the 'double wife'

existence with extreme distain and made no attempt to hide his disapproval.[2]

Basically, Lloyd George's clear mission, with no real party machine to back him, was to build up Allied supremacy in Flanders, bolstered in 1917 by American troop arrivals. This was notwithstanding the usual rounds of difficulties with the Admiralty over the convoy system and with the generals who equally, to varying degrees, distrusted and even despised politicians as a breed – invariably describing them as 'the Frocks' French military 'wobbling' in that year and the great German attacking thrust through northern France in the spring of 1918 nearly wrecked the overall Allied strategy – a strategy that nevertheless still involved a huge loss of British Infantry manpower, which greatly occupied Lloyd George's mind. These details do not concern this present financial based assessment, yet Lloyd George no doubt already, as will be seen, had ideas of money-making by way of his official war memoirs, in his head. As Prime Minister, he was well aware of his unique and privileged position to command information, facts, after dinner talks and personal recollections to be used for literary purposes and profit. He also had the clear support of his wartime confidants, Maurice Hankey and Philip Kerr[3], plus his champion 'note taker', later the faithful Principle Private Secretary, A.J. Sylvester. This was his official title, at Sylvester's own insistence, when he returned to work for Lloyd George in 1923. He had been awarded an OBE in 1918, followed by a CBE in 1920 but he was never awarded the Knighthood he craved.

Peter Rowland, in his masterly 872-page study devotes a whole separate chapter to, 'the man who won the war 1916-1918' to conclude, 'he [Lloyd George] had devoted himself, body, heart and soul to one supreme objective and that objective had now been achieved: whatever else may be said about him, no one could deny that he had played a major part in reaching it'.[4] As the First World War came to a close,[5] Lloyd George's mind was coming around to his political future thereafter. Financially, according to Donald McCormick 'Lloyd George's income from investments during the [Great] War had increased substantially ... his simple life of earlier days had given way to a more spacious and opulent way of living'. Effectively a three-point plan was considered; firstly, the governing arrangement with the Unionists must continue somehow, embodied in what became known as the 1918 'coupon' General Election. Secondly, a national newspaper must (as a political voice for Lloyd George) be acquired (this was particularly relevant, as by 1922 the press barons Northcliffe, Rothermere, Beaverbrook and later Riddell all lined up against him). Finally, and most importantly, funds must be obtained for future political purposes; for the new political grouping to continue the wartime's coalition ideals or better still, as Lloyd George would see it, to form a single effective party to combat socialism, even bolshevism.

After the expected post-war (i.e. after 11 November 1918) arguments about whether the Kaiser should be hanged or whether to 'make the Germans pay' [war indemnities and debts], Lloyd George looked forward, with his personal Premiership confirmed in the 1918 General Election, to a period of calm, calculated statesmanship by way of the Treaty of Versailles in Paris. To many colleagues, his short-tempered snapping and snarling of the later years of the war had given way to good humoured, patient, witty and conciliatory mannerisms, especially towards anything with a Welsh connection, however small. Even so, his long-term friendship with Churchill was under pressure, as was his relationship with his golfing partner and trusted press confidant, Lord Riddell (himself created a Baron for past services in 1920).[6] Additionally, his political base and fortunes were effectively in the hands of the Conservatives, now holding most seats in the new post-war House of Commons. Accordingly, the first part of Lloyd George's post-war triple plan was in place. Almost at the same time, the second objective fell into place, namely a newspaper acquisition.

Information via the Chief Whip, Freddie Guest, reached Lloyd George to convey the detail that Frank Lloyd, owner of the Coalition-friendly *Daily Chronicle* wanted to sell. By late 1918, a deal was struck; Lloyd George with full editorial policy now had his own newspaper, at a cost of £1.65 million. The purchasers, in a syndicate, included, mainly, Sir Henry Dalziel, Lord Inverforth, and most especially the Lloyd George Political War Chest or 'The Lloyd George Fund' as it was now beginning to be described. The editor, Robert Donald, and the military correspondent, General Maurice, were both immediately replaced.[7] In H.A. Taylor's biography (1951) of Robert Donald (d. 1934), the word 'resigned' is used to reflect his departure, whilst

D. McCormick in *The Mask of Merlin* contends (p.233) that as Lloyd George had a profound dislike of Donald, he was sacked.

The third part of Lloyd George's ambitious scheme, namely the Lloyd George Political Fund, expanded, as payments for national honours, especially coveted peerages, would now come into prominence. This block of money (invariably referred to as a 'fund' and later still a 'trust') was essentially a large deposit of money and other assets under Lloyd George's effective control. This was despite there being 'appointed trustees'. Such a cash pool came prominently to the fore after Lloyd George's departure from office in 1922. Some schools of thought believed that the fund had a suspected existence going back to the beginning of Lloyd George's premiership in 1916. Lloyd George's Chief Whips, Freddie Guest (1875-1937) and then Charles McCurdy (1870-1941) together with Sir William Sutherland (1880-1941), Lloyd George's press agent, were heavily involved. The fund itself was not generally available to the Liberal cause at election times, although Lloyd George did make some donations from 1923, for Liberal candidates' election expenses, particularly where radical and progressive candidates and their policies existed. In the 1923 electoral contest the Liberals fielded a large number of candidates yet disappointingly, success was limited and the Liberals did not achieve outright power. By 1924, the Liberal cash flow was at a low ebb, as was morale, and the General Election results left the Liberals with a vast reduction in seats. The author, Peter Rowland, asserts that these individuals had, 'been responsible for building up Lloyd George's Political Fund by the sale of honours on a massive scale'.[8] With a whiff of (as yet unproven) improper behaviour, even corruption, in the air, the Monarch, George V, was also becoming increasingly suspicious of some of the names put forward for ennoblement. Apparently, knighthoods were sold off for £10,000; baronetcies higher, at £30,000; and other peerages such as viscountcies and dukes even commanded £50,000 upwards. This was the Prime Minister 'hard at work establishing an independent position'.[9]

With more buffeting from striking miners and policemen, International Treaty creations, the Russian Bolshevik wars and the Asquithian Liberal movement, Lloyd George, with Margaret, left for a well deserved holiday break in Deauville, France. Riddell, who arranged for the holiday let by the sea, also accompanied them with the later additions of Eric Geddes, Sir Hamar Greenwood and his wife, Captain Ernest Evans (a secretary), Waldorf and Nancy Astor, Balfour, Bonar Law, General Allenby, Horne and Freddie Guest and, even later still, Lloyd George's wartime right hand men, Maurice Hankey and Philip Kerr. Invariably, at such gatherings, Lloyd George never had any money so his principal secretary, A.J. Sylvester, acted as his trusty unofficial banker! One can imagine minimal, if not zero, relaxation for Lloyd George, although his holiday was undoubtedly sweetened when the news came through that Andrew Carnegie, the American industrial millionaire and philanthropist, had died on 11 August 1919, leaving Lloyd George £2,000 a year for life in his will,[10] in recognition of Lloyd George's war services to the nation. Just weeks later, there was even more good financial news for Lloyd George. On 18 October 1919, Riddell presented Lloyd George with a cheque for £2,750, specifically for him to purchase a motor vehicle. It would seem that Frances Stevenson prompted this act of generosity in the wake of the Government's financial decision that Ministers were no longer to use official Government cars, and thus save public money. Despite these much pleasing personal financial events, the loyal, yet undiscriminating admirer Philip Kerr, later (from 1930) to become Lord Lothian (1882-1940), believed mid-1919 was the turning point in Lloyd George's political career, due to his renunciation of a moderate war reparations policy preceded by his deference to an angry telegram from 370 Conservative Members of Parliament.[11]

At the same time, Lloyd George yet again was changing properties. The house at Walton Heath, gifted to Lloyd George earlier, had now been disposed of for £7,000 and a new house acquisition, The Firs, at Cobham, Surrey, had been completed earlier in the year.[12] However, this new property in some ways never really appealed to him, although he had, as yet, little opportunity to properly inspect the house and enjoy same as he was so engaged in his House of Commons speech preparations. In turn, this asset was passed on to his son, Richard Lloyd George, once Lloyd George himself had decided to move out. The search for the ideal affordable property thus continued (at this very stage, Frances Stevenson had seen the estate in Surrey near Churt, with its 60 acres, which was on the market for £3,000 and was very enthusiastic that Lloyd George should proceed with this acquisition). The property, on the Surrey/Sussex and Hampshire borders, once acquired, was named Bron-y-De [Southern Crest] and was set in heathland heather, with sandy soil and woodlands. It was later discovered that the property faced north and not south as Margaret had first thought, leading to the house being incorrectly named Bron-y-De instead of Bron-y-Gogledd but, by then, it was too late to change the name. The renowned architect Philip Tilden was engaged to make suitable design and architectural changes. There was a new creation of a large open-hearth fireplace in the main library room, where, in the course of time, Lloyd George installed his high comfortable chair, which he later dictated his war memoirs from, in the 1930s. Later adjacent land was acquired so that the total acreage became 700 and then 850 acres in all.[13]

Separately, there was talk of financially remunerative war memoirs now in the air. Indeed, the American publishers, Messrs. Funk & Wagnall, had offered a total of £90,000 for these to be serialised in the *New York Times*[14] and the *Chicago Tribune*, with separate rights in the United Kingdom being managed by Cassells – sizeable money indeed! Elements of the press, the *Yorkshire Post*, *Morning Post*, and *Daily Mail*, ran editorials largely condemning this concept, and comparing the failure of obtaining war reparations from Germany with the apparent transparency of newspapers willing to pay Lloyd George for his memoirs. In the event, with added pressure from Maggie, Lloyd George released an official Downing Street statement to the effect that the said £90,000 would be donated to war relief charities. A few weeks later, an advance payment was made available of £5,500 although, with the public pledge now made to donate book profits to charity, Lloyd George's literary enthusiasm seemed to melt away, only to resurface ten or more years later when the monetary basis was different. Maggie's written summary was 'I did tell you not to take the money, didn't I? You can write another book to make money but not on the war. I would not touch a penny of it'.[15]

Internationally, the Rapallo Treaty and the much heralded Genoa Conference filled all the newspaper headlines of 1922. On 19 October that year, at the Coalition Conservative afternoon meeting at the Carlton Club in London, Stanley Baldwin spoke out very strongly against the perpetuation of the coalition arrangements and was quite offensive about Lloyd George. Lloyd George was left with no basis for continuing and resigned the Premiership of Great Britain, having earlier been expelled from the Liberal Party. It was a cruel blow. Frances Stevenson firmly believed 'the Asquith women are of course at the bottom of it [his removal]'.[16] He was, effectively, a man with little or no major party backing. Money scandals lay waiting in the wings, dominated from 1922 by the 'cash for honours' crisis.

In the meantime – leaving aside any monetary benefits from the Lloyd George Political Fund – with no ongoing Prime Ministerial salary, Lloyd George's official Parliamentary remuneration was reduced to the £400 salary per year as a Member of Parliament. Overall, some studies, such as Peter Rowland's, believe he was, nevertheless, comfortably off, yet Lord Kenneth Morgan contended he was a 'comparatively poor man, until 1928, by the standards of most politicians of the time' – a somewhat debatable verdict![17] Potentially lucrative offers, fortuitously, began to be received for his memoirs, often with sizeable sums of money mentioned. Frances Stevenson recalls his earlier words, 'I would not mind resigning; if I could become editor of *The Times* [net sales deficit about £3,000 per week] at a decent salary and with a decent contract'. Had Lord Rothermere secured *The Times*, Beaverbrook observed, it was his intention to put Lloyd George in as the editor and with control of policy.[18] However, this did not happen. There was even an unsubstantiated rumour that Lloyd George was, with 'friends' (i.e. the Lloyd George fund), wishing to make an offer for this newspaper – any such move was thwarted by an anti-Lloyd George faction converting *The Times*' ownership into a trust, permanently safe from acquisition.[19]

Rather than commit himself to such a gigantic task now, Lloyd George did agree to write a series of articles for the United Press Associations of America (UPAA). Its London representative proposed a series of fortnightly articles, which through the UPAA would be syndicated on a worldwide basis. Financially this would be on an equally shared footing with a reserve on the British rights to Lloyd George's writing. This arrangement would proceed. With Frances Stevenson retained on a 10 per cent profit share basis, with no attached salary, by the end of 1922 the latter was given a cheque for £3,000, thus representing £27,000 for Lloyd George. Hot on the heels of that came a slightly less attractive offer of paid articles for world circulation by the quite separate Associated Press of America, and this arrangement lasted until late 1939.[20] The earlier, very successful, visit to the United States and Canada greatly helped to boost Lloyd George's image and thus interest in these articles, plus, when at these overseas places, there was the additional fascination, for the public, of Maggie and Megan. A.J. Sylvester, the newly appointed Principle Private Secretary was also present.

Peter Rowland calculates that in Lloyd George's first twelve months as a journalist and writer, he managed to earn £30,000 (a situation touched upon in the earlier chapter) and with these earnings, plus the £2,000 Carnegie annual bounty, he was clearly able to afford the acquisition of 10 Cheyne Walk on the Chelsea embankment as a London home (this was after residing at 86 Vincent Square, a house made available under a temporary lease granted by Sir Edward Grigg with a rental of 16 guineas each week).[21] Additionally, Lloyd George was extending the acreage of the Churt estate by constantly adding small parcels of adjoining land, bought from immediate neighbours. It would therefore seem unlikely that any of the Lloyd George Political Fund monies were needed or indeed used for this quite personal expenditure.

As money was now coming in, with some regularity in sizeable amounts, the previous and relentless pressure to achieve financial security was much reduced, although far from eliminated. The new horticultural adventure, undoubtedly creating a huge challenge, revealed some throwback to the gardening tasks that Lloyd George undertook as a young boy, for his widowed mother. In some ways there had been a full turn of the wheel.

Notes

1. Private dinner engagement, November 1918. A.J. Sylvester, The Real Lloyd George, (Cassell, London, 1947), p.12.
2. Peter Rowland, Lloyd George, op. cit., p.417.
3. Frances Stevenson believed Kerr to be 'the most Christ like man' she had ever known. A.J.P. Taylor (Ed.) Lloyd George: A Diary by Frances Stevenson, (Hutchinson, London, 1971), p.214.
4. Peter Rowland, Lloyd George, op. cit., p.459.
5. Donald McCormick, The Mask of Merlin, op. cit., p.233.

6. By early 1919 Riddell was to view, in contrast, Lloyd George as "aristocratic and more intolerant of criticism". He was to finally break with Lloyd George in 1923 after the famous dog growling incident – with Riddell affixed motionless in terror at the Walton Heath House by Lloyd George's Airedale dog, Bill, for at least an hour before Lloyd George, roaring with laughter, rescued Riddell. Peter Rowland, Lloyd George, op. cit., p.638.

7. Andrew Cook, Cash for Honours, (The History Press, Stroud, 2008), pp.58-59. See also Trevor Wilson, The Downfall of the Liberal Party 1914-1935, (William Collins, 1966), pp.127-128.

8. Peter Rowland, Lloyd George, op. cit., p.575. Governments had, of course, sold honours long before Lloyd George but nothing like as extensive a scale.

9. Ibid., p.448.

10. Ibid., p.514.

11. J.R.M. Butler, Lord Lothian, (Macmillan, London, 1960), p.83 and p.199.

12. Frank Owen, Tempestuous Journey, op. cit., p.697

13. A.J. Sylvester (Ed. Colin Cross), Life with Lloyd George, (Macmillan, London, 1975), p.17. Also Ian Ivatt, Journal of Liberal History (46), Spring 2005, p.26.

14. See A.J.P. Taylor (Ed.), Lloyd George - A Diary by Frances Stephenson, (Harper & Row, London, 1971), p.242. The entry for 22 June 1922 reads, 'Last Friday [16 June 1922] Marshall, a representative of the New York Times came to see me ... I think they will make a substantial offer. Butterworths had earlier offered £40,000.'

15. David Lloyd George, The Truth About The Peace Treaties, Vol.I, (Gollancz, London, 1939), pp.404-416.

16. A.J.P. Taylor (Ed.), Lloyd George - A Diary by Frances Stephenson, op. cit., p.246.

17. Donald McCormick, The Mask of Merlin, op. cit., p.234. Equally, according to Trevor Wilson, The Downfall of the Liberal Party, op. cit., p.268, Lloyd George had come out of the Coalition Government with a 'party' fund exceeding £1 million, while The Liberal Asquithians (the 'Wee Frees') had now little or no money.

18. Stephen Koss, The Rise and Fall of the Political Press in Britain (Vol. 2), (University of South Carolina Press, Columbia SC, 1984), p.402.

19. K.O. Morgan, Lloyd George, op. cit., p.161.

20. Frances Lloyd George, The Years that are Past, (Hutchinson, London, 1967), pp.209-211.

21. John Campbell, If Love Were All, (Jonathan Cape, London, 2006), p.255.

5

1923-1930
The Mysterious Lloyd George Fund

'[The Lloyd George Fund] is not in the least a party fund in the usual acceptance of the term. The usual party fund represents an accumulation of gifts made through the Party Whip for party purposes. My fund does not represent any gifts made to any party'.
Lloyd George, in a letter to Lord Reading.[1]

With Lloyd George out of office, the two General Elections of 1923 and 1924 took place without any substantive Liberal challenge. The official Liberal Party funds, being separate, were at an all time low, even though Lloyd George agreed to make £100,000 (later claimed to be £160,000) from his 'Fund' available for election purposes. After the 1924 contest, it was clear that the successful Tories would possibly govern for most of the next five to ten years, with the short-lived Labour administrations in 1924 and 1929-31 being the first electoral signs of Labour replacing the Liberals. Yet financial issues now emerging were to dominate the immediate future for Lloyd George, and to underline the dispirited and demoralised state of the much reduced Parliamentary strength of the official Liberal Party there were now only 40 Liberal seats, 415 Conservative, 152 Labour and others, 6. The Liberal decline was to last until 1929, and, of course, there was no great improvement even then.

There was also an exchange of letters between Andrew Bonar Law, the Conservative Prime Minister, and Lord Edward Fitzalan, which suggested that Lloyd George, as opposed to the Liberal Party, might well have received up to £80,000 as money that originated from Lord Astor, originally set aside to cover, at least in part, the 1923 General Election expenses. If this allegation was correct, Lloyd George had indeed come into further vast sums of money.[2] It all made good reading, if nothing else. Looking ahead, but in the same vein, a much larger fund, with more politician involvement, was realised after the 1924 General Election by way of the sale of the *Daily Chronicle* newspaper. The matter was so complicated, with a number of schemes being floated and considered by the shareholders, that it was not until 1926 that the final terms received full shareholder approval. The shareholder base itself was limited but included the Lloyd George family (at one stage Gwilym was a salaried board member, after he had been defeated in Pembrokeshire in the 1924 General Election), Henry Dalziel (Lloyd George's principal agent), and Lords Bute, Inchcape and Inverforth (formerly Andrew Weir). Lloyd George attempted to secure a place for Frances Stevenson on the board in 1926 but this caused such an unholy row in the Lloyd George family that the proposal was dropped in consequence (see Appendix 3). Since the original *United Newspaper* share purchase in 1918, shareholders, on disposal, became 'a good deal richer as a result'.[3] Frank Owen in his brilliant tome, *Tempestuous Journey* asserts,

> 'Lloyd George then sold 614,003 *United Newspaper* 1918 Ordinary Shares for which he received a total of £2,888,642; paid as to £1,743,307 in cash and to £1,145,335 in £1 ordinary shares. He later agreed to pay £100 towards preliminary expenses'.[4]

One year later, in the late summer of 1928, the *Daily Chronicle* Investment Corporation stock was sold to the Inveresk Paper Company for an assumed figure of £2,500,000, comprising of £2,000,000 in cash plus a block of Inveresk paper shares, whilst retaining some *Daily Chronicle* Investment Corporation stock.[5] These were huge sums at the time.

Subsequent to Lloyd George losing power in October 1922, logically, as already intimated, he would invariably seek ways to return to power. Almost everyone, from King George V downwards, expected, if not hoped, at the time of his departure in 1922 that Lloyd George would return to a position of power one day. Could he either form a new party, perhaps of the centre, thus attracting possible support from both the existing mainstream Liberal or Tory groups, plus an infusion of successful business tycoons, or, on a national interest basis, would another Lloyd George-led Coalition Government be a superior alternative? Whichever of these near future options might prove practicable, the now continuing MP for Caernarvon Boroughs would need major funding and, with no current party machine behind him, it was an acute disadvantage he must overcome.[6] Such a fund could be achieved at a relatively low level by contributions from personal admirers or genuine gifts, plus receipts from hopeful men looking for some privileged route into lower Government posts and the Civil Service. Included in the types of contribution were payments made, as already implied, for honours and titles. This is where the large cash inputs would be most felt. There was a historic precedent here in particular, as the Stuart Kings, Pitt the Younger and Walpole all enriched themselves by selling titles, but by Victoria's reign this money-raising method was condemned; Lord Palmerston firmly supporting his Monarch's stance, agreeing with the Queen that weakening the genuine aristocracy constituted almost a heresy. Lloyd George, with his original background ethics and experiences of criticising privilege in his younger days, seemingly set out, quite deliberately, to encourage and extend the sale of honours into an effective 'racket'. This does not mean that, previously, the Tory and Liberal Parties were totally innocent of exploiting this system – they were not – but Lloyd George's 'honours' candidate selection methods knew no bounds. Some businessmen had made large fortunes during the 1914-1918 War and what better, from their viewpoint, than to purchase a title by virtue of substantial war equipment, etc., profits. Accordingly, further Viscountcies, Baronies, Baronetcies, and Knighthoods were lavishly acquired, to the fury of existing members of the House of Lords and to the serious worry of the King, George V, whose constitutional task was to confirm the Honours Listings submitted to him. Nevertheless, what shortly became known as the great 'honours scandal' was now very much a talking point, indeed murmurings about the lavishness of dispensing 'Birthday' and 'Prime Minister's' or 'Retiring List' honours had been a sizeable political issue, at least since June 1922.

The Duke of Northumberland (1880-1930) weighed in, via the House of Lords with a claim that

'The Prime Minister's party, insignificant in numbers and absolutely penniless four years ago [1918] has in the course of those four years amassed an enormous party chest, variously estimated at anything from one million to two million pounds'.[7]

Lloyd George's whips, Freddie Guest (1875-1937) and then Charles McCurdy (1870-1941), together with Sir William Sutherland (1880-1949), aided by honours 'touts' – shady commission-paid men, such as Robert Wells and Maundy Gregory – had effectively been responsible for building up the so called Lloyd George Political Fund (to the particular annoyance of the main Liberal Party Asquithians). Newspaper proprietors or editors, thus unofficial Downing Street outlets, were especially prominent in honours awards such as Max Aitken, later Lord Beaverbrook (*Daily Express*) 1917, Northcliffe (*The Times* and *Daily Mail*) 1917, Burnham (*Daily Telegraph*) 1919, Rothermere (*Daily Mirror* and *Sunday Pictorial*) 1919, Sir Edward Russell (*Liverpool Daily Post*) 1919, Riddell (*News of the World*) 1920, and Dalziel (*Reynolds News*) 1920, plus a whole host of lesser newspapermen. Northumberland went on to produce written evidence in the shape of correspondence reflecting offers of knighthoods for cash *from a Government Minister*. Legitimate questions were raised as to why Sir Joseph Robinson (previously fraudster and swindler), Sir William Vestey (First World War 'profiteer' and tax avoider), Sir James Waring (former managing director of a bankrupt business) and Sir Archibald Williamson (charged with trading with the enemy in the First World War – allegations later withdrawn), were offered peerages. One example of this is the alleged cost for Waring 'one way or another...£100,000'. Similarly, Northcliffe was supposed to have paid up to £200,000 for his title, half of which went to Mrs. Keppel and the other half to King Edward VII.[8] Although Robinson, once his background became public knowledge, withdrew his name. In total, by 1922, ninety peerages had been awarded, fifteen Barons a year created, 294 Knighthoods doled out, plus 25,000 of the newly-introduced Order of the British Empire awards.[9] The question is, how much did they each pay? In the early 1920s, the fund size could well have been nearly £4 million (Vivian Phillipps, a future Liberal Whip, estimated its extent at £3 million)[10] although estimates vary, starting at £1.5 million.

As has been noted, concerns were mounting as to the suitability of some involved for financial reasons, there was also the question of applicants' matrimonial irregularities. Lloyd George seemed to ignore growing protests over the lavish and indiscriminate honours awards – yet the monarch, George V, the Tory Party, Labour politicians and mainstream Liberals protested about the flagrant disregard for the basic background principles of awards. It was all down to recognition of services rendered in the war, Lloyd George hastily explained. Additionally, as Lloyd George was quick enough to point out, whilst the Political Fund existed, it was, nevertheless, under his effective control, although 'trustees', namely J.T. Davies, later Sir John Davies, Sir William Edge, Gwilym Lloyd George and Charles McCurdy were the governing body – at least notionally.[11] The funds were accumulated for the furtherance of specific political objectives, such as Lloyd George's much favoured policy committees. Indeed any such situations that Lloyd George cared to nominate! Quite specifically this fund was not, in any way, connected to or any part of the main Liberal Party (Asquithian) group and their funding arrangements – although the latter were somewhat impoverished by 1924. It could be construed that the fund, technically, belonged to no party. Payments received for past privileges (usually peerages) had been donated to Lloyd George (personally) and even after his premiership ended he still retained control although theoretically, as already implied, the trustees (in reality Lloyd George's personal nominees) retained full management control. This fundamental difference is vital to appreciate.

Nevertheless, the mere existence of a 'war chest' outside of main political party influences, let alone control had, for some time now, led to bad feeling, even recrimination, within the Liberal Party. In reply to the former Prime Minister Lord Rosebery's enquiring letter to *The Times* of February 1927, with later associated articles in editions of the *Morning Post*, and supportive responses from the *Daily Mail*, Lloyd George's office chose to issue a statement attempting some clarification:

'The fund which Mr. Lloyd George controls was raised in a way that does not differ from that followed by the Conservative Party or by the Liberal Party in the days before [wartime and beyond to the 1922] Coalition ... and all along it has been devoted to legitimate party purposes'.[12] Lloyd George added that he had 'not [ever] spent a penny of it [the fund] for his personal use', even adding the names of the administering trustees.[13]

This ongoing concept was turned on its head when, following the 1929 General Election, the former Foreign Secretary (1905-1916) Lord Grey, effectively now an arch enemy of Lloyd George claimed the entire fund for the cash-strapped Liberal Party, only to be refused on the grounds that the fund was operated personally by Lloyd George! It was, he argued, his to do whatever he chose, as Lloyd George emphasised when contacting his old colleague from the Marconi days, Marquis Reading (previously Sir Rufus Isaacs), as has been seen, on 14 August 1929. Conflictingly, Sir Donald Maclean, writing to Lord Gladstone on 30 July 1929 indicated that (in his view) 80 per cent of the Liberal contested seats in the 1929 General Election, 'must have received assistance, in whole or part from the Ll.G. Fund for the Election'.[14] A good deal of the fund was spent, certainly up to 1930, on financing Lloyd George's pet social investigations, largely ineffective in electoral terms yet the committees of enquiry once established did a very thorough job, at least, and produced substantial detailed reports which remain of some interest, even today, enquiring into coal, land, industry and national reconstruction in general. Equally, certain Liberal Party election expenses were paid out from the fund, but not all. Indeed John Campbell summarises, at least politically, that the fund did Lloyd George more harm than good.[15]

To some extent, politically, a form of natural progression had gathered pace over the 1920s. Asquith (Prime Minister 1908-1916) lost his Paisley seat in the House of Commons in the 1924 General Election, but later accepted a peerage as the Earl of Oxford and Asquith, obtaining a Knight of the Garter in 1925, whilst retaining the party leadership until after the 1926 General Strike. Lloyd George, out of office from 1922, retained his 'independent' party offices at 18 Abingdon Street, London (only a few seconds walk from the official Liberal Party headquarters at 21 Abingdon Street), whilst promoting the quite independent editorial line in his beloved *Daily Chronicle*, differing from the Liberal Party position. Gwilym Lloyd George, the second son of David Lloyd George and Dame Margaret (in 1920, during her husband's premiership, Margaret was appointed Dame Grand Cross of the Order of the British Empire [DBE] after raising over £200,000 for war charities), joyously for his parents, was first elected to Parliament in 1922 as an Independent Liberal for Pembrokeshire. However, he lost his seat in the 1924 Conservative avalanche. Megan Lloyd George, the youngest of the five Lloyd George children, entered politics by capturing the Anglesey Constituency in the General Election of May 1929, shortly after the Equal Franchise Act of 1928 had extended the vote to women aged 21 to 30 years of age, becoming the first female MP in the history of Wales. Megan retained the Anglesey seat right through until the General Election of 1951, when she was defeated by the Labour Candidate, Cledwyn Hughes. Lloyd George was immensely proud to have a son and a daughter sitting beside him in the House of Commons. Lloyd George greatly admired her, undoubtedly happy at this turn of political events, whilst his eldest daughter (Mair Eluned), who tragically died in 1907, never left his thoughts.

Nevertheless, Lloyd George became the Chairman of the Liberal Members of Parliament and the by now ailing Asquith resigned the Liberal Party leadership on 16 October 1926, in the wake of the General Strike, to subsequently die on 15 February 1928. Lloyd George succeeded Asquith as the Liberal Party leader, albeit in a scenario of Liberal disunity (Asquith's followers readily soured); a poisoned attitude with the Conservative Stanley Baldwin and the Labour leader, Ramsay MacDonald; existing distrust in the post-General Strike era and the ongoing squalid arguments over the Lloyd George Political Fund.

Financially, the entire Lloyd George family was not that hard-up at all (the so-called loss of Dame Margaret's pearl necklace in 1925 with an estimated value ranging between £600 and £1,000 – dependent upon which newspaper is read – gives one example and another is when Lloyd George made the decision to give his son-in-law, Olwen's husband Tom Carey-Evans, £1,000 to help furnish his medical consulting rooms in Wimpole Street. Tom's salary at the time, from the Indian Medical Board, was £600)[16] and, as will be evidenced in the next chapter, the highly remunerative First World War memoirs published between 1933 and 1936 would be equally controversial, plus the follow-up publications entitled *The Truth about the Peace Treaties*, a most substantial two-volume work published in 1938. Running parallel with these memoirs and beyond was the development of Lloyd George's fruit farming and attendant agricultural endeavours, which would involve huge capital expenditure and subsequently, a source of additional income receipts.

Notes

1. Dated 4 August 1929, Lloyd George Papers, Beaverbrook Library G/16/10/5, now held in the Parliamentary Archive in the House of Lords, London
2. W.M. Aitken (later Lord Beaverbrook), *The Decline and Fall of Lloyd George*, (Collins, London, 1963), pp.298-391, the Bonar Law and Lord Fitzalan Letters.
3. Frances Lloyd George, *The Years that are Past*, op. cit., p.219.
4. Frank Owen, *Tempestuous Journey*, op. cit., p.694. These newly acquired shares were in the newly formed *Daily Chronicle* Investment Corporation in 1927.
5. Ibid., p.694.
6. Peter Rowland, *Lloyd George*, op. cit., p.591. Lloyd George wrote to Maggie, 'I am working for a break, two or three years hence, after we have formed a Centre Party with a strong progressive bias'.
7. Frank Owen, *Tempestuous Journey*, op. cit., p.626.
8. John M. McEwan (Ed.), *The Riddell Diaries*, op. cit., p.368.
9. Peter Rowland, *Lloyd George*, op. cit., p.576, and Donald McCormick, *The Mask of Merlin*, op. cit., pp.235-243.
10. Dr. J. Graham Jones, *David Lloyd George and Welsh Liberalism*, op. cit., p.263.
11. See House of Lords, Lloyd George papers, G/16/3.
12. John Campbell, *Lloyd George - The Goat in the Wilderness*, (Faber & Faber, London, Reprint 2013), p.173. Also press statements issued 17 February 1927 and published in *The Times*, *Morning Post* and *Daily Mail*, 26 July to 16 August 1927.
13. Ibid., p.173.
14. Lloyd George papers, G/16/10/45, Beaverbrook Library, now in the Parliamentary Archive in the House of Lords.
15. John Campbell, *Lloyd George - The Goat in the Wilderness*, op. cit., pp.176-177.
16. Olwen Carey-Evans, *Lloyd George Was My Father*, op. cit., p.139.

6

1931-1945
Finances in Retirement

'It was his [Lloyd George's] proud boast that, 'I have grown two or three apples where there was only one thistle before and ten potatoes where there was only one dock' – but the fact that he had ample capital with which to experiment and adopt the most modern methods made him fail to realise that every other farmer could not do likewise between the wars'.

Donald McCormick[1]

After 1922, as has been seen, Lloyd George's Parliamentary isolation was not totally devoid of influence. However, after 1930, even this influence was on the wane – at least in Britain. Certainly, at the end of the 1920s, according to Lord St. Davids, the Lloyd George Fund stood at £765,000 (although some expenses had yet to be settled as regards the 1929 General Election) plus 279,000 *Daily Chronicle* shares. The annual income of the fund, after tax, was about £30,000. A particular outstanding deduction amounted to £6,750 and this was described as for 'personal arrangements'. The fund was not, as Lloyd George informed Rufus Isaacs, the Marquis of Reading, a party fund at all.[2] Interestingly, after Lloyd George's death in 1945, the Inland Revenue decided that the said 'fund' was not a personal asset and thus would not be included for Estate Duty calculation purposes. Separately, Lloyd George's personal assets were not insubstantial. He held, at least in 1930, a selection of equity shares, and also owned an expanding country estate in Churt, Surrey (where he and Frances effectively resided) and as his Welsh base, Brynawelon, (always recognised as Dame Margaret's house) in Cricieth, north Wales – in reality, his country retreat. There was also the leased property at 2 Addison Road, Kensington, London, acquired in 1927, in which he jointly resided with Margaret. Interestingly, in Dame Margaret's will of 1936, the Addison Road property is shown as a residential address and not as an asset, passing down. In Lloyd George's 1943 will there is no mention whatsoever of this property, because it was only leasehold.[3]

Politically, Lloyd George was now effectively partyless, as the Liberal Party was split in three different directions, and with his own family grouping of four now having little political clout or authority. The time, late 1931, was therefore ripe for a money-making venture. After touring the Great War battlefields in 1929 and playing host to the Indian leader and politician Mahatma Gandhi in 1931, Lloyd George was still recovering from an earlier prostate removal operation performed at Addison Road. He took with him Maggie, Megan and the redoubtable Principal Private Secretary Sylvester, sailing in the SS *Cormorin*, heading for the warmer climate, to convalesce in Ceylon (now Sri Lanka).[4] Meanwhile, Frances Stevenson and Malcolm Thomson were left behind to sort out the Great War papers, from 1914-1916, in readiness for Lloyd George's return to London to start the initial work on his war memoirs; although his written style needed some uplift – later to become flowing and easily readable.

In the foreword to the revised new edition of 1938, Lloyd George clearly explains the thrust and ongoing framework of his endeavours, namely,

'I am to tell the naked truth about war as I saw it from the conning tower at Downing Street. I saw how the incredible heroism of the common man was being squandered to repair the incompetence of the trained inexperts (for they were trained not to be experts in the actualities of modern warfare) in the production of equipment, in transport, in tackling the submarine menace, in the narrow, selfish and unimaginative strategy in the ghastly butchery of a succession of vain and insane offensives'.[5]

Another motive for embarking on this massive tome was to counter criticisms of himself already contained in the published reminiscences of some military war leaders including Haig, Kitchener, Asquith, Fisher, Jellicoe, Ian Hamilton, John French, William Robertson, and especially Lord Edward Grey. It presented an opportunity to portray Lloyd George's version of events in the Great War and in so doing, to settle old scores.[6] Lloyd George pressed on, convinced as ever of his urgent need to produce income from his writings, plus his inbuilt belief that he left politics as a relatively poor man! He undertook the actual writing himself whilst the background research was left, in the main, to Frances Stevenson, A.J. Sylvester and Malcolm Thomson. It is worth noting here that Malcolm Thomson was to be the official biographer of Lloyd George, his book being published in 1948, with the full co-operation of the Dowager Countess and full access to the papers that Lloyd George had left to her in his will. Additionally, Captain Basil Liddell Hart was engaged to explain specifically and, where appropriate, clarify, British Army matters. He was, moreover, complimentary to Lloyd George when expressing his comments on the great man's writing. War Office Cabinet papers were consulted, interviews conducted, Government archives inspected and other personal recollections examined. It was a massive research operation, including the review of Lloyd George's own retained Government papers – using the Churt property as a headquarters or base for these endeavours. Lloyd George had retained a large number of Government and Cabinet papers from when he fell from office in 1922. He really had no right to have these at all. These papers are now located at the Parliamentary Archive in the House of Lords.

Frances, not unnaturally, devoted her whole available time to Lloyd George's insatiable quests for wartime information for these memoirs, yet managed at the same time to organise her own private property acquisition, Heathercourt at Worplesdon, which was about twenty miles from Bron-y-De at Churt. Frances comments in her own published, edited diaries, 'I must say these [war memoirs] volumes are shaping into a fine and impressive piece of work' although she had some critical reservations over Lloyd George's character assessment of Winston Churchill, a section that was subsequently watered down in the final writing.[7] Even so, Frances never really warmed to Churchill, 'believing him to be cold and self engrossed'.[8] Separately, Sylvester's own role and difficulty is adequately explained or at least recorded in his diary entry for 21 November 1932:

'I started to go through them [papers] in the hundreds, if not thousands ... frankly he [Lloyd George] had given me no clear idea of what he wanted [or] what I was to look for and I was puzzled to know what Thomson and Frances had been doing in this ragtime Churt set up. LG has an aptitude of sending one on a wild goose chase'.[9]

Confusion also reigned over Thomson's instructions – was he, or Frances, to research the section on 'National Factories' and again Sylvester summarises, 'there are pieces of chapter all over the place, in a most disorderly fashion ... the way LG works is simply staggering ... I have never seen such a mess as there is at Churt'.[10] Leading politicians, including Baldwin and MacDonald, were shown drafts of the near-finished work, as was Lloyd George's brother William. King George V's authorisation of the manuscript was also sought, effectively via Prime Minister Ramsay MacDonald. Lloyd George's proposed book was not simply another historical analysis of events of the war and its aftermath – as the content was undoubtedly to defend Lloyd George's controversial wartime record and, indeed, to some extent presented auras of resentment, even rivalry in the war period. Lloyd George's portrayals of Grey, Haig and Kitchener were harsh, and once the King had studied the draft works, he did request some revision of the hurtful references to Ramsay MacDonald – an approach that only half persuaded Lloyd George to modify his words before completion. Nevertheless, the magnificent literary effort finally came into being in 1933 at about 200,000 words for the first two volumes, covering up to 1916, although Lloyd George and Frances had a sizeable debate, if not argument, over the level of royalties and advance payments that might be exacted from the publishers. Additionally, extracts from the *War Memoirs* were serialised in the *Daily Telegraph* no doubt generating further payments.

In sales terms, Lloyd George's memoirs were, despite reservations, and coming in the immediate wake of Lord Riddell's[11] published war memoirs, a considerable success. There were many who were impressed with the level of the researched supporting documentation to underpin Lloyd George's arguments, drawing unsolicited and warm praise from some historians of the day. As Lloyd George eloquently put it, 'I am not writing history as a historian but as a solicitor in possession of the documents'[12] – effectively to vindicate his wartime decision-making and reputation. Sales exceeded initial expectations, undoubtedly boosted by distribution through major British towns, cities, and in the main colonies of South Africa, Canada, Australia, and other geographical areas such as Egypt, Japan, China, Shanghai, plus almost all other European countries, except Russia. London hotels joined in the rush to satisfy customers' requests, as did the Royal Automobile Club and, naturally, the National Liberal Club.[13]

The first publications, covering the years 1914-1916, were most notable for the attack on the Foreign Secretary, Lord Grey, and cost £1 per volume, appearing in two-volume editions (1 and 2) dating from September 1933 and again in 1934. After the initial launch, extracts from *War Memoirs* began to be serialised in the *Daily Telegraph*. Separately, *The Times'* most reasonable analysis followed:

> 'It is fair to say that he [Lloyd George] has endeavoured to guard against palpable bias but he has failed whenever his hostility to some individual was deep rooted'.[14]

The *Telegraph* serialisation excerpt rights yielded £25,000 for Lloyd George. Further two-volume editions were published in 1936 with a cheaper complete edition appearing in 1938. Volume 3 of Lloyd George's memoirs was published in September 1934, relating to the 1916 Wartime Coalition Government and for the greater part covering naval matters as regards the U-boat menace and the installation of merchant navy convoys. Also included was the Neville offensive in France and America's eventual entry into the war in 1917. Naturally enough, the naval matters greatly incensed the Admiralty and Lords Jellicoe and Carson in particular. More serialisation of this work appeared, immediately, prior to publication in the press. *The Times* reviewer, again,

'Mr. Lloyd George has old scores to settle off and rarely makes a point without a jibe ... his bitterness affects his pen'.[15]

Kingsley Martin of the *New Statesman and Nation* was more generous and suggested there was manipulative skill in the work, yet urged forgiveness for Lloyd George's 'one fault of always being in the right'.[16]

Up to 6,000 copies of volume 3 were available on publication day, thus exceeding by over 100 per cent the equivalent demand on publication of the two previous volumes. Andrew Suttie, in his book, *Rewriting the First World War*, reveals that the publishers, Ivor Nicholson and Watson, had reported that by early 1937 sales stood at 12,707 for volume 1, 10,720 for volume 2 and 8,971 for volume 3. The fourth volume, published in the autumn of 1934, pointedly contained Lloyd George's attack on Haig's involvement in the Passchendaele campaign, which was a veritable monologue of 'bitter invective and terrible anger' supported by a formidable array of evidence and witnesses statements. In particular,

'If generals are no longer under any necessity to join their men in an attack or even to go within the zone of fire, it is more incumbent than ever to exercise the greatest care in ascertaining the task they call upon their officers and men to carry through – apart from good generalship, the obligations of comradeship and of common decency demand it'.[17]

By September 1936, the fifth volume had been concluded. This related to the events of early 1918 and the question of unity of command. This was swiftly followed by the final, sixth, volume, covering the Maurice debate, the German retreat, and finally the 11 November 1918 Armistice. The controversial Lloyd George version of events (criticism of leading army commanders, although praise for the French Field Marshall Foch) in these volumes was nowhere near as far reaching as the fourth volume content of some two years earlier. Nevertheless, demand was, as before, most encouraging. By early 1937, sales of volume 4 totalled 9,413 with sales of volume 5 reaching 6,607 and 5,819 for volume 6. Both the main and separate trade editions of the six volumes (all six volumes costing 20 shillings) totalled over 100,000 by mid 1938, and by 1944, sales of the first volume totalled 145,146 with 141,283 copies sold of volume two.[18] Readers' reactions ranged from shock at the bitter attacks on renowned war leaders and concern at the 'unrestrained, blatant assaults on individuals' to Lloyd George 'defending his own record of 1914-1918'.[19]

In immediate specific financial terms, the British rights brought Lloyd George £50,000 (as already seen, the *Daily Telegraph* yielded £25,000 of this as serialisation rights) and the quite separate American rights brought in $12,000. The quite separate two-volume follow-up work, *The Truth About the Peace Treaties*, later produced £9,000 for the British rights, $2,000 for the American rights and, some years later, an accumulation of book royalties achieved £3,000 from Russia, which in total generated £65,000.[20] According to Kevin Theakston in his 2010 book, *After Number 10*, 'In the five years from 1937, Lloyd George made a total of £43,000 from his journalism. The advances, royalties and newspaper serialisation earnings from his *War Memoirs* in the 1930s added up to something like £65,000 (equivalent to £2.4 million today)', which could confirm the above analysis.[21]

The year 1936 (August) also saw Lloyd George's much documented month-long visit to Germany with Megan, Gwilym, Professor T.P. Conwell-Evans (to act as translator and go between with Hitler), and Sylvester, to be joined later by Tom Jones and Lord Dawson (physician to Lloyd George and also the Royal Physician). As is well known, Lloyd George fell under the spell of the *Führer*; something he would greatly regret later. That November, Lloyd George departed, this time with Frances Stevenson, young Jennifer, Sylvester and his wife, for what he regarded as a well-earned holiday that lasted three months in Jamaica. Dame Margaret and Megan were to arrive later, which in turn would reflect in the immediate departure of Frances. Apart from the numerous games of golf, Lloyd George spent that time in the West Indies on his separate literary project – *The Truth about the Peace Treaties*, which in turn would yield more royalty income. Interestingly, A.J. Sylvester reveals some figures of Lloyd George's income from articles as follows, the figures apparently being calculated by Lloyd George's accountant, Mr. Walter Belcher:

1937	£14,800
1938	£3,600
1939	£11,500
1940	£7,200
1941	£6,600

Thereafter, royalty income came in at a comparative trickle with, for example, the sum for 1942 totalling, only £100. However, quite separately, Lloyd George received a commemorative casket and separate cheque for the sum of £660 to mark his half century as a Member of Parliament, by courtesy of the Welsh Parliamentary Party. Additionally, Lloyd George had a financial adviser, a Mr. John Wynford Phillips, who was the former Member of Parliament for Mid-Lanarkshire and, separately, Pembrokeshire. Phillips was also chairman of the Lloyd George Political Fund at one stage, and according to Lord Kenneth Morgan, Phillips' papers 'mysteriously disappeared'.[22]

The second major financial commitment during (mainly) the 1930s was Lloyd George's horticultural and farming experiments, and associated activities. Ever since the tract of hilly land, later Bron-y-De, was first acquired from the estate of Lord Ashcombe at Churt[23] in 1922 (when Lloyd George was aged 59) and from the outset of ownership, Lloyd George clearly sensed, despite the sandy soil, the possibilities of some serious agricultural involvement. With more time on his hands now that he was rather on the sidelines of political life, he seized the opportunity. To some extent, agriculture generally was in the doldrums in the 1920s, but in the next decade and even into the Second World War period, agriculture became a highly protected, organised and Government-subsidised occupation. The swing away from cereal crops to dairy produce, meat and fruit farming entirely suited the landowning former Prime Minister, especially relevant to his liking for soft fruit. Not only that, but with the acquisition of surrounding farms and land, the estate, only forty-five miles from London, increased to approximately 850 acres of which 300 were used for horticultural purposes and much of the remainder developed or rented out, seeing Lloyd George's capital reserves put to good use. Because there is little exact irrefutable evidence to support the concept, it is a matter of conjecture as to whether he might have used some or even a major part of the Lloyd George fund to buy some personal property at Churt, although it would appear unlikely. Nevertheless, Sylvester's written account does give us some clues, namely with monies coming out of the Lloyd George fund partly to financially support political costs, and equally in part to pay for personal holidays and expenditure on land and buildings on the Churt estate. In each instance, Lloyd George apparently did not wish Gwilym to know the exact detail; a little odd, bearing in mind he was a trustee.[24] The likely average agricultural acreage price during the 1920s and 1930s in the Surrey, Sussex, and Hampshire areas was about £100 per acre, yet it could reach as high as £200. This would mean that after the original sixty acre purchase in 1922, the remaining 800 acres at £100 per acre would therefore be £80,000, although this would ignore any attendant extra costing for existing farmstead buildings, other rural storage barns, farming equipment, the erection or improvements of farm workers' cottages etc.

For larger surrounding farms acquired, such as Jumps or Devils Jumps, such assets would invariably include existing tenanted properties, with rents receivable being anything between a few pounds per annum up to over £10 (see Appendix 6).[25] From a social viewpoint, more localised labour was used and Lloyd George reputedly paid above the minimum agricultural wage, which after the First World War was fixed in the southern region of England at approximately 25 shillings a week, going up to £2.5s a week, dependent upon the precise area and tasks required. The total number of men employed, at least up to the time of his death, numbered just over eighty men, thus implying a total weekly workforce wage in excess of £100.[26] In the Second World War years some of the workforce would undoubtedly have been conscripted into the forces, and replaced by a large number of 'land girls'. This in turn could have changed the workforce weekly wage bill. In the early days of his ownership, owing to his limited experience, separate sheep and cattle farming proved less than successful, although the poultry and pig endeavours eventually turned in some reasonable profits. Overall, net operating losses would have been incurred, although to some extent the tax treatment of farming losses, in accordance with the 1918 and 1926 Finance Acts, would possibly have given Lloyd George some favourable tax relief treatment. A.J. Sylvester, in his book *Life with Lloyd George*, gives us some clear figures for the farming results in the year 1938. Income from the farm was £6,030 with expenditure set at £11,534, i.e. a deficit of £5,504.[27] Clearly fortunes changed with the onset of wartime, as A.J. Sylvester remarks that, 'Lloyd George's farm, or what he called his 'food production' unit was being made to pay, and handsomely' detailed in his earlier 1947 book, *The Real Lloyd George*.[28] In support of this, a report from the *Surrey Beekeepers'* magazine archives indicates, from a correspondent now resident in Herefordshire, that 'Lloyd George made a fortune as a middle man, buying up potatoes and other vegetables grown [on his estate] for the war effort and selling them for a profit to the army in Aldershot. I recall an aged character in plus fours with wild hair and a Welsh accent!'[29]

Therefore, as money was effectively not a problem, it was easy enough to buy in expert assistance in order to show those who doubted his agricultural and horticultural endeavours a thing or two. In farming techniques he really only had a hazy notion of the concepts involved and thus recognising this, was not slow in calling in the experts from the nearby Wye Agricultural College, the East Malling Research station (principal, Sir Ronald Hatton) and Surrey County Council, to set him on the right path; soil content and manurial values took priority. Apples, pears, plums and his much favoured cherries came forth in some abundance together with the much heralded 'Lloyd George Raspberry'. By 1935, his land produce was entered into a soft fruit show and Lloyd George secured the first, second and third prizes for his blackcurrants, plus a silver cup. This was presented by the National Farmers Union, Kent Branch, Fruit and Vegetable Committee. Separately, his specialist brand of Cox's apples was sold through the prestigious firm of Harrods in London.[30] However, Lloyd George was undoubtedly a difficult man to work for. A number of farm managers came and went, the fourth being a Mr. Coles. On Lloyd George's return from Jamaica, Coles indicated to Lloyd George that he wanted to leave, basically because he did not like the so-called [im]moral atmosphere of the place, and more relevantly Coles told Lloyd George that nobody would make the farm pay for itself, as long as Lloyd George continually interfered with the management of the business and the day-to-day events.[31]

Despite these successes, neighbouring farmers and growers still had grave misgivings about the crop yields produced on what they regarded as a light, scrubby and sandy soil. Lloyd George would confound them all. Mrs. Ann Parry, Lloyd George's secretary, librarian and archivist now stationed at Churt, later was appointed bee-keeper with her existing portfolio of duties. She recalls one particular eight acre orchard with the apple varieties being Cox's Orange Pippins and Gladstones, Grenadiers, Bramleys, James Grieve, Beauty of Bath, Lane's Prince Albert, Rivals, Ellison Orange, Annie Elizabeth, Worcester Pearmain and Laxton Superb being planted in long rows of twenty trees in each, and all growing handsomely. The orchard foreman had a complete 'orchard plan' in the adjacent shed. The secret was, of course, in the soil preparation; mustard seed was sown in the first year, lupins in the next, followed by heavy ploughing of green manure. Bees were then needed to carry pollen to and from other apple varieties to fertilise the apple blossom itself.[32]

Equally, there was the question of irrigation. Luckily a nearby water diviner, a Mrs. Wylie (a lady of Scottish descent who lived in a nearby caravan) was discovered and managed to find substantial water reserves under Lloyd George's extensive estate. In due course, once an electric pumping station was installed, some 12,000 gallons of water an hour was dispersed across the orchards by an overhead system of watering. In 1939, a new local irrigation scheme were additionally installed, costing in excess of £3,000, with Dame Margaret Lloyd George visiting for the much publicised official launch celebrations. Such an event on a former Prime Minister's farmed land attracted an entire legion of press men, photographers and journalists – a moment of immense satisfaction for them both. The entire enterprise was organised on a grand scale so that fruit was regularly and continuously collected throughout the farming year. There were several large glass houses, fruit stores, and an extensive marketing pavilion (known as the Lloyd George Farm Shop) on the main road outside. Locals acquired their fruit and vegetables there, as did many greengrocers and trades people.[33] As already mentioned, Lloyd George's knowledge included the question of keeping and the value of bees, vital in the pollination process. He gained a minimum level of understanding of the subject and by the mid-1930s joined the British Beekeepers' Association and, a little later, the Scottish Beekeepers' Association. The latter was presided over by the famous Dr. John Anderson (University of Aberdeen), under whose guidance the now expanded Bron-y-De hives were strengthened. Extra bee stocks were obtained from a reputable breeder in southern France; the total number of hives now spread around the entire estate reaching thirty. The 1936 summer weather conditions were the best for many years and the Lloyd George hives, masterminded by Ann Parry, produced an average of sixty-eight pounds of honey each – winning a national first prize in the process. That same year, Lloyd George was asked to provide the opening address at the National Honey Show at Crystal Palace. Such an excellently high honey yield was not repeated again until the wartime year of 1943, when Lloyd George was eighty years of age. At that time, a ton and a half of honey was garnered. Lloyd George was especially proud of his sales of honey directly to Fortnum and Masons and Harrods, both leading, top-class London stores.[34] A.J. Sylvester reports that Lloyd George made the following comments:

> 'When I go to my hives I regard myself as one of the greatest employers of the best workmen in the country. There is no looking at the clock to see whether it is lunchtime. There are periods of enforced idleness even amongst bees. When they have no food, you must give them the dole, and not too much means test, they are just standing in the market waiting for the sun to tell them that there is a job waiting for them. Honey is good for the old, it is very good for young children … I know it, I feel it after I have taken a feed of honey. I am then ready for anything or anybody'.[35]

As is evident, Lloyd George was immensely proud of the achievements undertaken on his estate and took great pleasure in walking through the orchard of blossoming fruit trees, in particular. Where the fruit was in the developing stage, he would walk through the orchards sometimes more than once a day – morning and evening, simply assessing the blossoms and counting the fruit set; to later calculate the likely fruit-crop commercial value and undoubtedly speculating on possible financial outcomes.[36] As the entire estate expanded, Lloyd George opened, from time to time, the quite separate Bron-y-De gardens to the public, with local charities being able to benefit; for example, in 1934 it was for Surrey Nurses. The standard entry cost was 1 shilling per head.[37] Jean Alys Campbell-Harris, born 1922, now Baroness Trumpington, summarises her less than lively life as a wartime land girl at Bron-y-De – her parents were friends of Olwen:

> 'Being at Churt was desperately dull, there weren't even any animals [that she came into contact with] here on the farm. It was all fruit. I picked apples, packed apples, and repacked apples. Each and every apple was wrapped in paper and then the apples were packed into bushel baskets. It was endless. Occasionally, to relieve the tedium I picked raspberries, the variety that was named after Lloyd George'.[38]

Separately, money was also found, in 1934, to settle on Frances, in the shape of a new wooden bungalow on the Churt estate, firstly called The Old Barn, which was a disused farm building and later let, but was re-named with an Arthurian touch, Avalon. This was to be Frances' own main home, replacing the Worplesdon property. Lloyd George now felt young Jennifer would be much geographically closer to him. He additionally urged Megan to build some farm cottages on the land he had given her at Churt, using the alleged housing shortage as a reason. Money too, somewhat untypically, was found to pay in 1937 for Sylvester's wife, Evelyn's, medical expenses – Lloyd George was not always generous with his employee's wives![39]

In addition to the (by now) thriving farming venture at Bron-y-De, Lloyd George made yet another farm acquisition, in August 1939, this time in Wales, on a hill between Cricieth and Llanystumdwy, undertaken during the Eisteddfod that year. The holding consisted of a Georgian mansion, Tŷ Newydd, with views of the sea and mountains, and thirty-seven acres, costing approximately £7,000.[40] The building was in a fairly run-down condition, with the former owner having sheep in the kitchen and the surrounding acres in a neglected and parlous state. Nevertheless, Lloyd George was determined from the outset to repeat his albeit expensive successful fruit growing activities in Surrey; after all the challenge was to draw up a war plan for food production, and this would also include wheat growing, fruit and Welsh Black cattle.[41] Experts, once again, were summoned, yet initially to no great avail: the first fruit crop yield from the 3,000 fruit trees planted – but staked too tightly – was, as A.J. Sylvester described, 'very poor – more for pigs than humans'.[42]

Further agricultural advisers were summoned, including a county horticulturalist, Mr. John Roberts. The farmhouse itself required sizeable repair and renovation and in this regard the respected architect, Clough Williams-Ellis (the creator of the Italianate village at Portmeirion) was brought in to supervise the large reconstruction, including a huge bay window that was installed in the library. At one point Mr. McDougal, the Churt farm manager, was despatched to Tŷ Newydd with a wagon load of furniture to add the benefit of his knowledge to the somewhat different soils of north Wales.[43] By 1942, the agricultural and orchard growing rescue scheme, including vast weed clearance, pruning costs and furrowing, had been completed. Lloyd George could indeed now show some of his local fellow farmers what could be done, albeit by successful cash injections – eight acres alone were devoted to successful fruit crops, although it needed some rows of poplar trees planted to create a windbreak, to assist growth to the fruit trees and vegetables. In that same year of 1942, two neighbouring farms came on the market, but sensibly enough Lloyd George declined (no doubt carefully considering the likely upgrading expenditure) to proceed to purchase, although his brother William, alternatively, was rather keen. Tŷ Newydd was demanding enough![44]

As will therefore be seen, Lloyd George lived out his last days at Tŷ Newydd with his second wife, Frances, his two cats, Juan and Blanco, together with Mrs. Bennett the housekeeper, with a gardener and farm worker being later added to the staff. Thus with the acquisition and subsequent commercial exploitation of two estates, now working farms, Lloyd George entered into his twilight years. He was aged seventy-six when the Second World War began in the summer of 1939. Politically, he was isolated yet still the elected member for Carnarvon Boroughs, a constituency he had retained, with Dame Margaret's never ending support, from 1890. For Lloyd George there would be no call for his wisdom at Government level; his poor relationship with Prime Minister Neville Chamberlain would ensure that. However, he was certainly very content, indeed, proud of his second son Gwilym (Member of Parliament for Pembrokeshire), as wartime in 1940-1945 saw Gwilym with a number of Government portfolios, namely Board of Trade, Ministry of Food, Ministry of Fuel and Power, and there was even talk of Gwilym attaining the speakership of the House of Commons, which came to nothing, and all these positions came and went.

As has already been mentioned, Lloyd George's second son Gwilym was privately educated at some of the best schools money could buy and was described as a good sportsman, especially at rugby and cricket. Gwilym was certainly not the most academically gifted student but still managed to win a place at Cambridge.[45] Lloyd George was superbly proud of his daughter Megan who, unlike her brother Gwilym, never held and indeed was never offered Ministerial office, but won the Anglesey seat for the Liberals in 1929 and was still the island's MP at the outbreak of the Second World War.

The ongoing proud images of Lloyd George with these high levels of family attainment were much cherished, although such ideals were hugely dented by the death of Dame Margaret after a fall at Cricieth, in January 1941. He was devastated beyond comprehension and even after marrying Frances Stephenson at Guilford Registry Office in 1943, albeit amidst significant opposition from his children, Dame Margaret continued to hold a sizeable place in his affections despite the couple having lived separate lives for over twenty-five years. After Dame Margaret's demise, Megan was left Brynawelon, in Cricieth. Lloyd George, somewhat tactlessly, then indicated that he was unable to afford to continue paying Megan an allowance for the upkeep of her property as he had done previously. Megan was more than upset and Sarah Jones, the long-serving family housekeeper, vowed never speak to Lloyd George again! Nevertheless, Lloyd George still continued to pay the five guineas weekly rent on Megan's cottage at at Chesham.[46]

This second marriage was brief, as his health was already deteriorating with his doctor, Dawson, diagnosing cancer, although not informing Lloyd George directly. His return to Wales at Tŷ Newydd would be his last pilgrimage, and there was a long and difficult goodbye to his house in Churt. He also realised he was too old and effectively enfeebled to contest Carnarvon Boroughs at the next General Election. It was not to be anyway, as he was offered an Earldom (Lloyd George of Dwyfor) which after some reflection he accepted in the New Year's Honours in 1945. As it transpired he was never to take his seat in the House of Lords (something he would have entirely dismissed as a young Liberal lawyer in the 1880s-1890s) as he was to pass away in the library of his Welsh farm, with his bed placed so that he actually had sight of his schoolboy home close by at Llanystumdwy, on 26 March 1945, aged eighty-two. His wife Frances and his daughter Megan were linked in a short temporary peace, with Frances holding his left hand and Megan his right, as he passed from this world to the next. Young, teenage Jennifer looked on from the foot of his bed, and surrounding the bed itself were Olwen, Ann Parry, Gwilym, nurse Thomas, Sarah Jones, Mrs. Bennett, Sylvester and Dr. Prytherch. Lloyd George's own physician, Dawson, had died only nineteen days previously. His elder son Dick was absent as he was receiving treatment for alcoholism in a sanatorium in Denbigh.[47]

There was, as had been said on previous occasions, 'no one quite like Lloyd George'.[48]

Tributes arrived from worldly figures; General Smuts, Sir Archibald Sinclair, Winston Churchill, to name but a few. Perhaps most pointedly, Aneurin Bevan firmly affirmed; 'We have lost our most distinguished member and Wales her greatest son'.[49]

The funeral was held on Good Friday, 30 March, 1945. Lloyd George had earlier made it abundantly clear that he wished to be buried in a spot marked with a large stone on the banks of the river Dwyfor, in preference to any other site, including the plot where Dame Margaret was interred. The coffin was placed on a hand cart, driven by Robert Evans, Lloyd George's aged friend, dating back to his childhood days. Even then, unbelievably, the entire funeral arrangements were subject to family bickering.[50] There was to be even greater squabbling when the financial terms of Lloyd George's will were revealed in full, his Probate being granted on 31 July, 1946 – see Appendix 5.

Notes

1. Donald McCormick, *The Mask of Merlin*, op. cit., p.314.
2. Frank Owen, *Tempestuous Journey*, op. cit., p.689. Letter from Lord St. David to Sir Herbert Samuel, dated 9 July 1929, and letter from Lloyd George to the Marquis of Reading, dated 14 August 1929.

3. Peter Rowland, *Lloyd George*, p. 686. Addison Road is referred to as 'his' house.
4. A.J. Sylvester noticed that in Lloyd George's baggage there was a huge trunk of books for background reading material relative to publications by Generals and other military people.
5. David Lloyd George, *The War Memoirs of David Lloyd George*, (Odhams Press, London, 1933-34), p.v.
6. Dr. J. Graham Jones, 'The Lloyd George War Memoirs', *Transactions of the Honourable Society of Cymmrodorian, new series*, Vol.14 (2008) p.1 (127/143).
7. A.J.P. Taylor (Ed.), *Lloyd George - A Diary by Frances Stephenson*, op. cit., p.264.
8. Countess [Frances] Lloyd George, *Frances – More than a mistress*, (Cromwell Press, Wiltshire, 1996), p.109. Peter Rowland, *Lloyd George*, op. cit., p.699, contends that Frances Stevenson's diaries were the main contribution she could make to Lloyd George's *War Memoirs*.
9. See Dr. J. Graham Jones, 'The Lloyd George War Memoirs', op. cit., p.7. Also the A.J. Sylvester papers, National Library of Wales, file E7 entitled 'How I helped Lloyd George write his war memoirs', pp.2-3.
10. Dr. J. Graham Jones, 'The Lloyd George War Memoirs', op. cit., p.22-23.
11. Later, after his death in 1934, Lloyd George was left £1,000 in Riddell's Will, as was Winston Churchill. It later transpired that Frances Stevenson was also left £1,000.
12. Andrew Suttie, *Rewriting the First World War – Lloyd George, politics and strategy 1914-1918*, (Palgrave Macmillan, London, 2005), p.12.
13. Ibid.
14. Dr. J. Graham Jones, *The Lloyd George Memoirs*, op. cit., p.9.
15. Ibid., p.11. Also Andrew Suttie, *Rewriting the First World War, op. cit.*, p.21, notes Baldwin wrote to Lloyd George - letter 19 April 1933 - professing his support and admiration, yet brother William George wrote to Megan Lloyd George - 14 May 1933 - worried about Lloyd George's treatment of Lord Grey. See Peter Rowland, *Lloyd George*, op. cit., pp.702-703. Conversely, Hankey later told Lloyd George - 2 April 1934 - that the chapter on submarines was wonderful –
16. Ibid., p.11.
17. Peter Rowland, *Lloyd George*, op. cit., p.709.
18. For all volume figures, see Andrew Suttie, *Rewriting the First World War*, op. cit., pp.12-13.
19. Dr. J. Graham Jones, *The Lloyd George Memoirs*, op. cit., pp.13-14.
20. Frank Owen, *Tempestuous Journey*, p.725.
21. Kevin Theakston, *After Number 10*, (Palgrave Macmillan, London 2010), p.128.
22. All figures taken from A.J. Sylvester (Ed. Colin Cross), *Life with Lloyd George* (Macmillan, London, 1975), p.313. Also see K.O. Morgan)Ed.), *Lloyd George - Family Letters 1885-1936*, op. cit., p.46, footnote.
23. For future references to Churt and Bron-y-de, see Olivia Cotton, *Churt Remembered* (self published, 2002), pp.75-79, and Anne Parry, *Thirty Thousand Yesterdays*, (Pennant Publishing, Camberley, 1977), pp.54-61.

24. A.J. Sylvester, *Life with Lloyd George*, op. cit., p.202 and p.213.
25. Per David Marshall, qualified Estate Agent and Valuer, of Messrs. H.J. Burt & Son, High Street, Steyning. Interestingly, in the mid-1930s as a young boy, David Marshall was taken by his father to Lloyd George's estate at Churt.
26. Alan Howkins, *Reshaping Rural England, A Social History, 1850-1925*, (Routledge, London, 1992), p.277.
27. A.J. Sylvester, *Life with Lloyd George*, op. cit., p.222.
28. A.J. Sylvester, *The Real Lloyd George*, op. cit., p.294.
29. Letters to the Editor of *Beecraft*, December 2005. Surrey Beekeepers' Archives, Woking, Surrey.
30. Peter Rowland, *Lloyd George*, op. cit., pp.745-746.
31. A.J. Sylvester, *Life with Lloyd George*, op. cit., p.182 and p.189. In fact Lloyd George was greatly upset that someone would suggest his farming was not run on business lines, and more resembling a hobby.
32. Ann Parry, *Thirty Thousand Yesterdays*, op. cit., p.54. Ann came from a farming family in Anglesey. She was first appointed as a secretary to Lloyd George's London office after a brief career in nursing.
33. Dr. J. Graham Jones, 'Lloyd George at 80', *Transactions of the Honourable Society of Cymmrodorion*, new series, Vol.16 (2010), pp.61-81.
34. Ann Parry, *Thirty Thousand Yesterdays*, op. cit., pp.62-65. The honey jars were labelled 'From the Estate of D. Lloyd George, OM, MP'. Also see John Campbell, *If Love Were All*, op. cit., p.207.
35. A.J. Sylvester, *Life with Lloyd George*, op. cit., p.155.
36. Frances Lloyd George, *The Years that are Past*, op. cit., p.238.
37. A.J.P. Taylor (Ed.), *Lloyd George - A Diary by Frances Stephenson*, op. cit., p.270.
38. Jean Trumpington (Baroness), *Coming up Trumps*, (Macmillan, London, 2014), pp.36-37. See also Appendix 8 for further land girl experiences.
39. John Campbell, *If Love Were All*, op. cit., p.428 and p.450.
40. Initially, the purchase was intended for his daughter, Olwen – Thomas Jones, *Lloyd George*, (Oxford University Press, Oxford, 1951), p.259. The cost price figure has been deduced by a record of a discussion between Frances Stevenson and A.J. Sylvester on 2 May 1944 – see A.J. Sylvester, *Life with Lloyd George*, op. cit., p.325.
41. Ibid.
42. John Campbell, *If Love Were All*, op. cit., p.494, footnote.
43. Ffion Hague, *The Pain and the Privilege*, op. cit., p.531, and Ann Parry, *Thirty Thousand Yesterdays*, op. cit., p.71.
44. Peter Rowland *Lloyd George*, op. cit., p.792, and Donald McCormack, *The Mask of Merlin*, op. cit., p.299.
45. Also, during Gwilym's life he had several directorships and for a time was a Justice of the Peace. His parents would be genuinely pleased and proud.
46. Dr. J. Graham Jones, *Journal of Liberal History*, (Issue 74, Spring 2012), pp.32-33.

47. John Campbell, *If Love Were All*, op. cit., pp.496-497, and A.J. Sylvester, *The Real Lloyd George*, op. cit., p.310.
48. *Hansard*, Aneurin Bevan – House of Commons, 28 March 1945.
49. Ffion Hague, *The Pain and the Privilege*, op. cit., p.537.
50. Ibid.

7

1888-1972
Frances

*'Frances should have been quite a wealthy woman, but her outgoings
were considerable – she never learned to be careful with money'.*

Ruth Longford[1]

Frances Louise Stevenson came into Lloyd George's life in 1911,
initially as a tutor for his daughter Megan, later to become his own
secretary and mistress for the next thirty years. After Dame Margaret's
death in 1941, Lloyd George married Frances in 1943. The story is
hugely more complex than that, yet to end the examination of Lloyd
George's financial dealings some brief notes on Frances' finances
appears more than merely appropriate. Frances was widowed at the
age of fifty-six and was to live until eighty-four; coloured by a period
of ongoing wrangling and bitterness by Lloyd George's children. In
accordance with Lloyd George's 1943 will, the executors finalised
as Gwilym Lloyd George, John Ernest Evans, and Frances Louise
Dowager Countess Lloyd George, Frances benefited by:

1. South Field Orchard adjoining Old Barn Lane at Churt and the
    growing fruit trees therein.
2. All papers and documents dealing with Parliamentary, political
    and war matters together with total copyright of the same.
3. The Village Institute (with some minor adjoining land) at
    Llanystumdwy – by later codicil.

4. The farmhouse and surrounding land at Tŷ Newydd, north Wales including both the farming deadstock and livestock, plus a garage – by later codicil.
5. A painting of Marrakech by Winston Spencer Churchill.

In addition to these assets, Frances had in her own name the property Avalon at Churt, as already referred to, which included a small farm and surrounding orchards – now a garden centre and tea rooms. Additionally, Frances was also paid the Carnegie Pension as Lloyd George's widow; at the same £2,000 per annum rate. In 1940, following the death of Colonel Tweed, a former lover, Frances was bequeathed £2,000 with an extra £500 for Jennifer (who also received a supplement of capital to an existing trust arrangement undertaken for her earlier). This is perhaps a strong indication that Jennifer was Tweed's and not Lloyd George's daughter, as he left nothing for her in his will.

Some authors attribute characteristics of Frances to include a certain level of carelessness with money, meanness, completely self-interested behaviour and an offhand way of treating the Churt estate employees. As an example of these 'attributes', Dr. J. Graham Jones' article in the *Journal of Liberal History* (issue 74, Spring 2012, pp. 32-34) is worth re-reading.

George Dyer, Lloyd George's long-suffering chauffeur, had firm evidence, in 1942, that Frances was regularly diverting some of the coking coal supply intended for Bron-y-De to her own cottage at Avalon ... 'Miss Stevenson interferes with the domestic staff and is so mean to them'.

Moreover, Frances' sister Muriel was apparently added to the Bron-y-De payroll records as a 'land girl' with very little, if any, actual agricultural work being undertaken.

On the other side of the coin, Frances was a brilliant multi-linguist, a first rate confidential secretary, a diligent researcher and above all, over many years, had to put up with Lloyd George's various flirtations, indiscretions, moods and irritating habits.

Note

1. Ruth Longford, *Frances, Countess Lloyd George - More than a Mistress*, (Gracewing, Leominster, 1996), p.184.

Appendix I

Comparative Money Values

£100	in	1880	= £8410.64
£100	in	1890	= £8984.09
£100	in	1900	= £8593.48
£100	in	1910	= £8235.42
£100	in	1920	= £3124.90
£100	in	1930	= £4569.94
£100	in	1940	= £3913.86
£100	in	1945	= £3017.56

Source: Inflation Calculator at www.moneysorter.co.uk

Appendix 2

Lloyd George's Life Assurance Particulars

Copy of Northern Assurance life committee's minutes, dated 10 January 1895, showing Lloyd George accepted at normal rates as an insurable risk.

(Courtesy of Norwich Union [Aviva] Archives, Norwich.)

Appendix 3

The Lloyd George Family Meeting in 1926 – Summary

The Lloyd George family viewed this proposal as 'the final affront' and resolved to tackle Lloyd George on his relationship with Frances, who vividly recalled the episode when she came to pen her memoirs some forty years later:

> 'The Lloyd George family was incensed, and in 1926, when Lloyd George was in low water politically and many people were out for his blood, his family decided to tackle him on his relations with me. A joint letter was written, signed by his wife and all his children, demanding that I should be removed from his secretariat ... or else ... Lloyd George was enraged by the note, which he had received from his family. He then wrote a terrible letter to Dame Margaret, upbraiding her and the children for attacking him and offering her a divorce, which he said he would welcome. I knew nothing of all this until Lloyd George handed me the letter which Dame Margaret had returned to him, obviously accepting defeat. This was one of the many hurts I experienced, inevitably, in my confrontation with the Lloyd George family'.

Lloyd George, it is clear, did at least draft a very strong letter to his wife at this point:

> 'I know now too well what has been going on the last few days. G[wilym] in his new mood of ranting hysteria has told three or four persons all

the details of the 'family councils' which have taken place. It appears that my children are following the example of the children of Noah by exposing their father's nakedness to the world. It is not the reputation of Noah that has suffered. But his children have gone down the ages as first class skunks for turning on the old man. ... As to G[wilym]: I have offered him good terms & I do not propose to recede from them whatever the consequences. I will be neither bullied nor blackmailed. ... I must tell you how deeply pained I am to learn that you & Megan have turned against me. I have been for some time sick of public life. I work hard – very, very hard – and get nothing but kicks. I have been contemplating clearing out & writing my book in retirement. I propose on Thursday to tell them to find another candidate. I am an old man. I mean henceforth to enjoy the leisure, which is my due'.

But this letter, though harsh and perhaps unreasonable, does not ever refer to the possibility of a divorce, and, now that the leadership of the Liberal Party at long last lay within Lloyd George's grasp once again, it seems inconceivable that he would even have contemplated such an extreme step. He had always told Frances that he was not prepared to jeopardise his political advancement or career for her sake. As the letter was eventually published in *My Darling Pussy* in 1975, preserved among the correspondence between Lloyd George and Frances, it seems likely that Lloyd George, ever the wily operator, drafted the letter simply to placate Frances, then showed it to her but never in fact sent it to Dame Margaret. When the chips were down, Lloyd George was well capable of outwitting both the women in his life. The episode then soon blew over. The family backed down somewhat, Lloyd George gave up on his campaign to get Frances a seat on the board of the *Chronicle* and indeed soon sold the newspaper. Many members of the family made handsome profits from the sale. Frances had undoubtedly been hurt by the course of events, but the status quo had been preserved.[1]

Note

1. Dr. J. Graham Jones, "Lloyd George and Dame Margaret 1921-1941", *Transactions* (Caernarfonshire Historical Society), Vol.67, 2006, pp.98-127.

Appendix 4

Dame Margaret Lloyd George's Financial Background

Evidence of Margaret Lloyd George's (née Owen) financial position is hard to come by. Interestingly, Maggie's (Margaret) father, after due delay in agreeing to his daughter's marriage to David is to have said,

> 'I can't give her any money at the moment ... *only the money that she herself already has'*.[1]

By the early 1890s her father, Richard Owen, had retired from his prosperous farming and cattle valuation business and in accordance with his will dated 27 May 1887, all his 'property of whatever description' was bequeathed to his wife (Margaret's mother), Mary. Richard died on 2 November 1903 and Mary, the widow, passed away not long afterwards on 27 May 1907. Upon Mary's death, the property assets (together with any other residue) of the late Richard Owen, namely Brynawelon and Llys Owen in Cricieth, passed entirely to Maggie. There is some evidence of additional assets being in Maggie's name, as Richard Lloyd George, subsequently Viscount Gwynedd, recollects as a boy, his mother (Maggie) selling him her part interest in trading vessels going into and out of Porthmadog Harbour, by exclaiming 'two and three eighths' inches 'ownership' of such vessels'.[2] By 1913 Margaret Lloyd George is amongst the list of owners of the *Gestiana*, holding a 1/64th share in the vessel.

Equally her brother in law, William George, had 4/64th shares in the *Isallt*, a Newfoundland trader from 1909.[3]

Letters between David and Margaret Lloyd George also throw some light on Maggie's own finances, namely as Lloyd George writes from Genoa on 2 September 1892, 'I think you have done very nicely in purchasing that plot of ground, although we may be ill-able to spare the £150 which the purchase money and [surrounding] hedges will involve. This will also afford you an excellent opportunity to dress you much for the balance of the legacy'. Years later, in an undated letter, Lloyd George writes, 'I have just bought [you] 2500 shares in 'Chronicle'; had to pay £2650 for them ... [at] ...the end I put them all in your name. After all, my Will [not his last] leaves everything I have to you, nothing to the children, and certainly not to anyone else'.[4]

However, as will be seen from the official probate and will copy documents, numerous properties, all apparently in Cricieth, in addition to those already referred to, were owned at the date of Maggie's death on 20 January 1941.

Notes

1. Dr. J. Graham Jones, *Journal of Liberal History*, issue 63, Summer 2009, p. 29.
2. Viscount Gwynedd, *Dame Margaret*, George Allen & Unwin, 1947, pp.53 – 54.
3. Emrys Hughes and Aled Eames, *Porthmadog Ships*, Gwynedd Archive Services, 1975, pp.198 and 208.
4. N.L.W., 20442C (misc.).

Appendix 5

Lloyd George's Will, dated 12 November 1943 and the subsequent Codicil of 2 September 1944

Executors (original will)   Gwilym Lloyd George (son) and John Ernest Morris (solicitor) – also Trustees

Codicil   As before, plus Frances Louise Lloyd George, as further Executrix and Trustee

Beneficiaries (in order shown in the will)
Albert James Sylvester
Various female domestic servants
Ann Parry
Gwilym Lloyd George
Olwen Carey-Evans
Frances Louise Lloyd George
Megan Lloyd George
Trustees of the Village Institute of Llanystumdwy

Note 1
There is no mention of Lloyd George's first son, Richard (Dick), as Lloyd George believed he had financially assisted him many times over, during his lifetime.

Note 2
The Inland Revenue ruled that any monies held in the Lloyd George Political Fund (see Chapter 4) did NOT form part of Lloyd George's personal estate and thus the fund was excluded.

Note 3
Gross Value of the estate for 1946 Probate was £139,855 – a value in excess of £6.5 million today.

Appendix 6

Churt Estate Valuation

Purchase particulars of the Jumps (or Devils Jumps) estates sales agent's valuation of June 1935, showing the various agricultural and domestic dwellings contained therein, together with the tenancy terms and existing rental arrangements. Note the listing includes garages, a shop, and even a small wayleave rental for telephone poles in addition to an array of let dwellings.

The total value for purchase was as stated, £25,000, with an annual rent roll of nearly £1,200 (approximately £40,000 in 2015).

Source: Gillian Devine Papers (2014) now held in Farnham Museum and History Centre, Woking.

Appendix 7

Selected list of household furniture, plate, linen, books, as valued for Probate on 6 July 1945, as held at Bron-y-De, Churt, Surrey

Total value assessed £9,3,25 16s 6d

Note 1   Rolls Royce motor car included at £1,750 – registration plate no. CYP 922

Note 2   Cinematograph equipment – £300

Appendix 8

Testimony of Gwynne Chuter of Frensham, near Farnham, Surrey

I worked with two other 'land girls' in the [Bron-y-De] glasshouses, growing tomatoes, in the latter part of the [1939-1945] War. I started there a few days after Lloyd George's eightieth birthday [January 1943] celebrations – the workers from all the farm sections were gathered together for a photograph. By that time his presence was not in evidence very often. I do remember Miss Stevenson and her sister [Muriel] who lived in Churt for many years.

I cycled four miles each way to work [at the farm] in all weathers; I earned £2. 8s [£2.40] for a forty-eight hour week – the 8 shillings was deducted for National Insurance, etc. A lot of produce was sold at the [farm] shop – a log cabin built by Mr. Disney (the former Carpenter). Also Mr. Boniface drove the lorry for the wholesale produce. A land girl called Marie delivered [produce] locally by a pony, called Joey, and a small cart.

Source: Letter dated 27 March 2014, addressed to the author.

Bibliography

Manuscripts and Letters

National Library of Wales (NLW)
A.J. Sylvester (National Library of Wales)
Lord K.O. Morgan
Lord Tenby

Parliamentary, other archives, both national and local

Gladstone Archives
Brighton Street and Business Directory Archives, Brighton, East Sussex
Parliamentary Debates, House of Commons Library
House of Commons Information Office (Parliamentary Archives)
Lloyd George Papers, House of Lords

Personal Interviews

Eironedd Baskerville (translated from Welsh)
Mrs. Gwynne Chuter
Gillian Devine
Dr. Helen Doe
Dr. J. Graham Jones
Jennifer Longford
David Marshall

Other reference sources, articles, etc.

British Bee Keeping Association
F.W.S. Craig – *British Parliamentary Election Results* (Macmillan, 1974)
Dean Wilson (solicitors), Brighton
District Probate Registry, Leeds
Dulwich College Archives
Eastbourne College Archives
Ian Ivatt, *Journal of Liberal History*

Dr. J. Graham Jones, 'My War Memoirs of David Lloyd George', *Transactions of the Honourable Society of Cymmrodorion*, (2008), and 'Lloyd George at 80', (2010).
Journal of Liberal History
Lewes Golf Club
Manchester Guardian
Roedean School Bursary Records

Financial Institutions

Inland Revenue
Anna Stone, Group Archivist, Aviva (Norwich Union) records.

Books

Adams, R.J.Q.: *Balfour - The Last Grandee*, (John Murray, London, 2007)

Aitken, W.M. (Lord Beaverbrook): *The Decline and Fall of Lloyd George*, (Collins, London, 1963)

Blake, Robert, and Louis, William Roger (Eds.): *Churchill: a Major New Assessment of his Life in Peace and War*, (Oxford University Press, Oxford, 1993)

Bonham-Carter, Violet: *An Intimate Portrait*, (Harcourt Brace, New York, 1965)

Butler, J. R. M.: *Lord Lothian*, (Macmillan, London, 1985)

Campbell, John: *The Goat in the Wilderness*, (Faber and Faber, London, 2013)

If Love Were All, (Jonathan Cape, London, 2006)

Carey-Evans, Olwen: *Lloyd George was my Father*, (Gomer Press, Llandysul, 1985)

Carradine, David: *Aspects of Autocracy*, (Yale University Press, 1994)

Clifford, Colin: *The Asquiths*, (John Murray, London, 2002)

Cook, Andrew: *Cash for Honours*, (The History Press, Stroud, 2008)

Cotton, Olivia: *Churt Remembered*, (self-published, 2002)

Cregier, Don M.: *Bounder from Wales* - Lloyd George's Career Before the First World War, (University of Missouri Press, Columbia, 1976)

Cross, Colin: *Life with Lloyd George*, (Macmillan, London, 1975)

Donaldson, Lady Frances: *The Marconi Scandal*, (Quality Books, London, 1962)

Edwards, J. Hugh: *From Village Green to Downing Street*, (George Newnes, London, 1908)

The Life of David Lloyd George, (Waverley, London, 1913)

Grigg, John: *Lloyd George from Peace to War, 1912-1916,* (Methuen, London, 1985)

The Young Lloyd George, (Methuen, London, 1973)

Gwynedd, Viscount: *Dame Margaret,* (George Allen and Unwin, London, 1947)

George, William: *My Brother and I,* (Eyre and Spottiswoode, London, 1958)

George, W.R.P.: *Lloyd George* - Backbencher, (Gomer Press, Llandysul, 1983)

The Making of Lloyd George, (Faber and Faber, London, 1976)

Gilbert, B.B.: *David Lloyd George – A Political Life,* (Batsford, London, 1987)

Hague, Ffion: *The Pain and the Privilege,* (Harper Collins, London, 2008)

Hattersley, Roy: *David Lloyd George – The Great Outsider,* (Little Brown, London, 2010)

Hobson, Dominic: *The National Wealth,* (Harper Collins, London, 1999)

Jenkins, Roy: *The Chancellors,* (Macmillan, London, 1998)

Johnson, Boris: *The Churchill Factor,* (Hodder & Stoughton, London, 2014)

Jones, J. Graham: *David Lloyd George and Welsh Liberalism,* (National Library of Wales, Aberystwyth, 2010)

Jones, Mervyn: *A Radical Life - Megan Lloyd George 1902-66,* (Hutchinson, London, 1991)

Jones, R. Mervyn: *The North Wales Quarrymen 1874-1922,* (University of Wales Press, Cardiff, 1999)

Jones, Thomas: *Lloyd George,* (Oxford University Press, Oxford, 1951)

Koss, Stephen: *The Rise and Fall of the Political Press in Britain* (Vol. 2), (University of South Carolina, 1984)

Longford, Ruth: *Frances, Countess Lloyd George - More than a Mistress,* (Gracewing, Leominster, 1996)

Taylor, A.J.P. (Ed.): *Lloyd George, A Diary by Frances Stevenson,* (Hutchinson, London, 1971)

Lloyd George, Frances: *The Years that are Past,* (Hutchinson, London, 1967)

Lloyd George, David: *Lloyd George - The Truth about The Peace Treaties,* (Gollanz, London, 1939)

The War Memoirs of David Lloyd George, (Odhams Press, London, 1934)

Lloyd George, Richard: *My Father - Lloyd George*, (Crown, New York, 1961)

McCormick, Donald: *The Mask of Merlin*, (Macdonald, London, 1963)

McEwen, John M. (Ed.): *The Riddell Diaries*, (Athlone Press, New Jersey, 1986)

Morgan, K.O. (Lord): *Lloyd George*, (Purnell, London, 1974)

Lloyd George - Family Letters 1885-1936, (Oxford University Press and University of Wales Press, 1973

The Age of Lloyd George, (George Allen and Unwin, London, 1978)

Owen, Frank: *Tempestuous Journey*, (Hutchinson, London, 1954)

Parcq, Herbert du: *The Life of David Lloyd George*, (Caxton Publishing, London, 1912)

Parry, Ann: *Thirty Thousand Yesterdays*, (Pennant Publishing, Camberley, 1977)

Price, Emyr: *David Lloyd George*, (University of Wales Press, Cardiff, 2006)

Pugh, Martin: *Lloyd George*, (Longman, London, 1988)

Riddell, George (Lord): *More pages from my Diary*, (Country Life, London, 1934)

Roberts, Richard: *Saving the City - the Great Financial Crisis of 1914*, (Oxford University Press, Oxford, 2013)

Rowland, Peter: *Lloyd George*, (Barrie and Jenkins, London, 1975)

Simon, John (Viscount): *Retrospect*, (Hutchinson, London, 1952)

Suttie, Andrew: *Rewriting the First World War - Lloyd George and Strategy 1914-1918*, (Palgrave Macmillan, London, 2005)

Sylvester, A.J.: *The Real Lloyd George*, (Cassel, London, 1947)

Sylvester, A.J.: (Ed. Colin Cross): *Life with Lloyd George*, (Macmillan, London, 1975)

Theakston, Kevin: *After Number Ten*, (Palgrave Macmillan, London, 2010)

Trumpington, Baroness: *Coming Up Trumps*, (Macmillan, London, 2014)

Watkin Davies, W.: *Lloyd George*, (Constable, London, 1939)

Wilson, Trevor: *The Downfall of the Liberal Party 1914 – 1935*, (William Collins, London, 1966)

Index

NB Hyphenated names are indexed by the second element throughout

welsh academic press

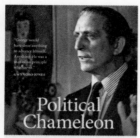

POLITICAL CHAMELEON
In Search of George Thomas

Martin Shipton

"I picked up this book expecting it to be a hatchet job, but it is a very fair book and a very well researched book. The problem with George Thomas is that one can write a book that is very fair and very well researched yet he still comes out of it very badly."
Vaughan Roderick, BBC Radio Wales

Drawing on previously unpublished material from Thomas' vast personal and political archive in the National Library of Wales, and interviews with many who knew him during his career, award-winning journalist Martin Shipton reveals the real George Thomas, the complex character behind the carefully crafted facade of the devout Christian, and discovers a number of surprising and shocking personae - including the sexual predator - of this ultimate *Political Chameleon*.

978-1-86057-137-4   304pp   £16.99   PB

'YOU ARE LEGEND'
The Welsh Volunteers in the Spanish Civil War

Graham Davies

'Excellent. A paean to the working men and women of Wales who went to Spain to fight in defence of the fledgling Spanish Republic.'
Keith Jones, son of volunteer Tom Jones from Rhosllanerchrugog

'Well researched, and using previously unpublished sources, 'You Are Legend' is recommended reading. It is important that the contribution of the large number of Welsh volunteers continues to be recognised.'
Mary Greening, daughter of volunteer Edwin Greening of Aberdare

'A highly readable and comprehensively researched account of the Welsh Brigaders.'
Alan Warren, Spanish Civil War historian

Almost 200 Welshmen and women volunteered to join the International Brigade and travelled to Spain to fight fascism alongside the Republican government during the 1936-1939 Spanish Civil War. While over 150 returned home, at least 35 died during the brutal conflict. '*You Are Legend*' is their remarkable story.

978-1-86057-130-5   224pp   £19.99   PB

welsh academic press

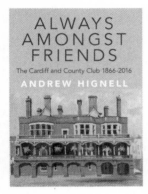

ALWAYS AMONGST FRIENDS
The Cardiff & County Club 1866-2016

Dr. Andrew Hignell

Since its establishment in 1866 by prominent businessmen and the gentry of south Wales, the Cardiff and County Club has played a central role in the commercial, political and sporting life of Cardiff, as it developed from a burgeoning Victorian coal metropolis into the dynamic Welsh capital city of today.

Extensively researched and lavishly illustrated, *Always Amongst Friends* not only traces the fascinating 150-year history of the Club through a scholarly study of the social and economic history of Cardiff, but also celebrates the Cardiff and County Club's colourful characters, their mischievous humour and exudes the warmth and camaraderie so treasured by its members.

978-1-86057-129-9   304pp   £20.00   PB

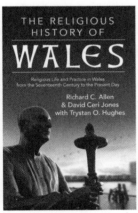

THE RELIGIOUS HISTORY OF WALES
Religious Life and Practice in Wales from the Seventeenth Century to the Present Day

Richard C. Allen & David Ceri Jones, with Trystan O. Hughes

An essential reference guide, this volume draws together an impressive collection of academics and religious practitioners to map out, for the first time, the religious multiplicity and diversity of Wales, manifested in the following religions, beliefs and denominations:

The Church in Wales -   Independents (Congregationalists) - Baptists
The Religious Society of Friends (Quakers) - Roman Catholicism Calvinistic Methodism - Wesleyan Methodism - The Moravian Church Unitarianism - Salvation Army - Pentecostalism - United Reform Church Seventh-Day Adventism - The Church of the Latter-Day Saints (Mormons) - Jehovah's Witnesses - Evangelicalism - Judaism - Islam Sikhism - Bahá'Í

978-1-86057-079-7   293pp   £25.00   PB

welsh academic press

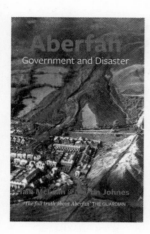

ABERFAN
Government and Disaster
(Second Edition)

Iain McLean & Martin Johnes

'*The full truth about Aberfan*'
The Guardian

'*The research is outstanding...the investigation is substantial, balanced and authoritative...this is certainly the definitive book on the subject...Meticulous.*'
John R. Davis, Journal of Contemporary British History

'*Excellent...thorough   and   sympathetic.*'
Headway 2000 (Aberfan Community Newspaper)

Aberfan - Government & Disaster is widely recognised as the definitive study of the disaster and, following meticulous research of previously unavailable public records - kept confidential by the UK Government's 30-year rule - the authors explain how and why the disaster happened and why nobody was held responsible.

978-1-86057-133-6   192pp   £19.99   PB

GARETH JONES
Eyewitness to the Holodomor

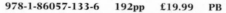

Ray Gamache

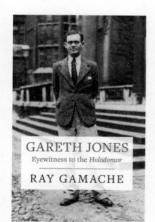

'*Excellent ... serves as a warning to journalists not to be taken in by official sources and political ideology but to report what they actually learn through their own efforts.*'
Prof. Maurine H. Beasley, Univ. of Maryland

'*...meticulously researched book [that] returns Gareth Jones to his rightful status, as one of the most outstanding journalists of his generation*'
Nigel Linsan Colley, www.garethjones.org

'*Extraordinary ... Jones' articles ... caused a sensation ... Because [his] notebooks record immediate impressions and describe events as they were happening, they have an unusual freshness ... Jones' reputation has revived thanks to the Ukrainian government's broader efforts to tell the history of the famine.*'
Anne Applebaum, The New York Review

Gareth Jones (1905-1934), the young Welsh investigative journalist, is revered in Ukraine as a national hero and is now rightly recognised as the first reporter to reveal the horror of the Holodomor, the Soviet Government-induced famine of the early 1930s, which killed millions of Ukrainians.

978-1-86057-122-0   256pp   £19.99   PB

welsh academic press

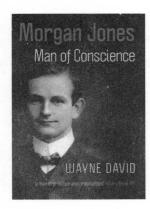

MORGAN JONES
Man of Conscience

Wayne David

'Wayne David deserves great credit for bringing Morgan Jones to life in this well-researched and very readable book.'
Nick Thomas-Symonds MP

'Wayne David writes of one of his predecessors as Labour MP for Caerphilly with the understanding of the political insider and the contextual knowledge of the historian.'
Professor Dai Smith

'Jones was a man of principle and pragmatism.'
Hilary Benn MP, from his Foreword

Imprisoned in Wormwood Scrubs for his pacifist beliefs during the First World War, Morgan Jones made history by becoming the first conscientious objector to be elected an MP when he won the Caerphilly by-election for Labour in 1921.

978-1-86057-141-1   128pp   £16.99   PB

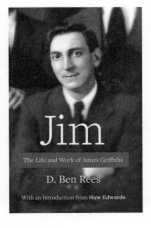

JIM
The Life and Work of Jim Griffiths

D. Ben Rees

'The remarkable story of James Griffiths takes us all the way from the origins of British Labour to the origins of devolved Wales. Ben Rees has crafted a highly-readable and authoritative account of the life and times of one of Wales' greatest statesmen'
Huw Edwards

In this, the first full-length biography of James Griffiths in English, Dr D. Ben Rees provides a comprehensive yet very accessible and personal study of one of the towering figures of twentieth-century Welsh and British politics. As Minister for National Insurance in the Atlee post-war government, introduced the Family Allowance in 1946 and became Secretary of State for the Colonies in 1950.

A product of the Welsh radical political tradition, James Griffiths became a miner at 13 and was a conscientious objector during WW1. He rose to become President of the South Wales Miner's Federation, the MP for Llanelli for 34 years, Chairman and then Deputy Leader of the Labour Party and the first Secretary of State for Wales in 1964.

978-1-86057-120-6   400pp

welsh academic press

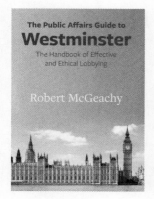

The Public Affairs Guide to
Westminster
The Handbook of Effective and Ethical Lobbying

The Public Affairs Guide to Westminster is the essential handbook for organisations seeking to influence legislation and shape policy development in the UK Parliament and at UK Government level, and is packed with invaluable advice on devising cost effective public affairs strategies and campaigns that achieve success on a limited budget.

Robert McGeachy's step-by-step guide - for private, public and third sector organisations - expertly strips away the mysteries and misconceptions of engaging with the UK Government, Opposition parties, as well as with individual MPs, Peers and the civil service.

The Public Affairs Guide to Westminster will empower campaigners to maximise their influence and to ensure their voice is heard at Westminster.

978-1-86057-134-3   224pp   £19.99   PB

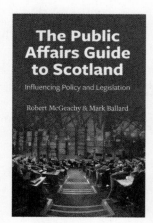

The Public Affairs Guide to
Scotland

'[an excellent] guide for the newcomer and a 'memory stick' for the expert. It contains all a person needs to know to engage with the Parliament, the Government, local authorities and civic society in an effective and efficient way. This book shows how one can participate in that fast moving and interesting field and will become a tool for all who wish to get involved and achieve success in their endeavours.'
Michael P Clancy

'Effective and informed activity by MSPs, the Parliament, the Scottish Government and third sector bodies in taking forward legislation and promoting causes, whilst protecting the most vulnerable is the best way to ensure a truly participatory, power sharing democracy and that is why this guide will be so useful ... Mark Ballard and Robert McGeachy, through the pages of this important book, are therefore doing democracy a service.'

Michael Russell, MSP for Argyll & Bute Professor in Scottish Culture & Governance, The University of Glasgow

978-1-86057-126-8   224pp   £19.99   PB